The Bible Index Pocketbook

Harold Shaw Publishers
Wheaton, Illinois

ISBN 0–87788–077–8

Cover photo: Robert McKendrick

Library of Congress Cataloging in Publication Data

The Bible index pocketbook.

    1. Bible—Indexes, Topical.
BS432.B464   220'.016   81-8940
ISBN 0–87788–077–8   AACR2

First printing, June 1981
Second printing, July 1981
Third printing, October 1981
Fourth printing, April 1982
Fifth printing, December 1982
Sixth printing, May 1983
Seventh printing, May 1984
Eighth printing, October 1985
Ninth printing, October 1986
Tenth printing, August 1988
Eleventh printing, June 1990

How to Use Your Bible Index

"All scripture is inspired by God and profitable for teaching . . . and for training in righteousness, that the man of God may be complete, equipped for every good work." (2 Timothy 3:16–17).

Have you ever wondered what the Bible has to say about certain topics like work, friendship, marriage? Or have you wondered who Jehu was, or what happened at Jericho? This index of the themes, places, and persons of the Bible can help you find the answers! It can give you a quick reference, like where to find the Sermon on the Mount, or it can lead you into an exciting exploration of a theme like forgiveness or evangelism. The Index can be used with any translation or paraphrase of the Bible.

Of course, *The Bible Index Pocketbook* is only a beginning. If you want to do further study on a topic, you will need to consult a Bible dictionary, a concordance, or a Bible commentary.

One word of caution: a verse should always be studied in its biblical context; isolating a verse may distort the intended meaning of the Bible passage. Also, for a more complete grasp of a topic, be sure to read each related entry given in parentheses after the primary topical entry; for example: Contentment (See also Anxiety, Peace).

The Bible Index Pocketbook will guide you into the exciting truths of the Bible. It will help you locate answers to your questions and will make you feel more at home with God's Word. Ultimately, you should learn to know its Author better.

Abbreviations in the Index

Old Testament

Genesis	Gen.	Ecclesiastes	Eccles.
Exodus	Exod.	Song of Solomon	Song of Sol.
Leviticus	Lev.	Isaiah	Isa.
Numbers	Num.	Jeremiah	Jer.
Deuteronomy	Deut.	Lamentations	Lam.
Joshua	Josh.	Ezekiel	Ezek.
Judges	Judg.	Daniel	Dan.
Ruth	Ruth	Hosea	Hos.
1 Samuel	1 Sam.	Joel	Joel
2 Samuel	2 Sam.	Amos	Amos
1 Kings	1 Kings	Obadiah	Obad.
2 Kings	2 Kings	Jonah	Jon.
1 Chronicles	1 Chron.	Micah	Mic.
2 Chronicles	2 Chron.	Nahum	Nah.
Ezra	Ezra	Habakkuk	Hab.
Nehemiah	Neh.	Zephaniah	Zeph.
Esther	Esther	Haggai	Hag.
Job	Job	Zechariah	Zech.
Psalms	Ps.	Malachi	Mal.
Proverbs	Prov.		

New Testament

Matthew	Matt.	1 Timothy	1 Tim.
Mark	Mark	2 Timothy	2 Tim.
Luke	Luke	Titus	Titus
John	John	Philemon	Philem.
Acts	Acts	Hebrews	Heb.
Romans	Rom.	James	James
1 Corinthians	1 Cor.	1 Peter	1 Pet.
2 Corinthians	2 Cor.	2 Peter	2 Pet.
Galatians	Gal.	1 John	1 John
Ephesians	Eph.	2 John	2 John
Philippians	Phil.	3 John	3 John
Colossians	Col.	Jude	Jude
1 Thessalonians	1 Thess.	Revelation	Rev.
2 Thessalonians	2 Thess.		

A

Aaron (See also Priest, Priesthood)

Family of   *Exod. 6:16–20; 1 Chron. 6:3–15, 50–53*
Spokesman for Moses   *Exod. 4:14–5:21; 7:1–2*
Consecrated priest with sons   *Exod. 28:1–29:46*
Fashions golden calf   *Exod. 32:1–6, 21–25*
Jealous of Moses yet repentant   *Num. 12:1–12*
Symbol of priesthood   *Ps. 115:10, 12*

Abandonment (See also Desertion)

Of this world for Christ   *Phil. 3:7–10*
■ Of men by God because of:
  Rejection of God   *Rom. 1:21–32*
  Sin   *Heb. 10:26–31*

Abednego (See also Meshach, Shadrach)

Youth captured by Nebuchadnezzar   *Dan. 1:1–7*
Saved in fiery furnace   *Dan. 3:1–30*

Abel (See also Cain)

Account of his life and death   *Gen. 4:1–8, 25*
The first victim of human sin   *Matt. 23:35*
Example of faith   *Heb. 11:4*
Compared with Christ   *Heb. 12:24*

Abigail

Wife of Nabal   *1 Sam. 25:1–38*
Wife of David   *1 Sam. 25:39–42*

Abihu

Son of Aaron   *Lev. 10:1*
Killed after offering unholy incense   *Lev. 10:2*

Abijah
King of Judah   *1 Kings 15:3*
Made war against Israel   *2 Chron. 13:1-20*

Abishai
Helps David spy on Saul   *1 Sam. 26:5-12*
One of David's mighty men   *2 Sam. 23:18-19*

Abner
Commander of Saul's army   *1 Sam. 14:50*
Fights against David   *2 Sam. 2:8-32*
Aligns with David   *2 Sam. 3:8-21*
Murdered by Joab   *2 Sam. 3:27*

Abomination (See also Evil, Sin)
Idolatry   *Deut. 7:25-26*
Sexual immorality   *Lev. 18:1-30*
Dishonest trade   *Deut. 25:13-16*
Sorcery   *Deut. 18:9-13*
Lies   *Prov. 12:22*
False worship   *Isa. 1:10-15*

Abomination of Desolation
Prophecy of   *Dan. 8:11-14; 9:27; 12:11*
Mentioned by Christ   *Matt. 24:15; Mark 13:14*

Abortion
Soul of fetus is implied   *Ps. 51:5; 139:13-16*
Penalty for killing fetus   *Exod. 21:22-25*

Abraham (See also Covenant, Sarah)
His history and God's call   *Gen. 11:27-12:7*
Involvement with Lot   *Gen. 13:1-14:16; 18:16-33*
Encounter with Melchizedek   *Gen. 14:17-24*
Covenant established with God   *Gen. 15:1-21*
Fathered Ishmael by Hagar   *Gen. 16:1-16; 21:8-21*
Circumcision covenant introduced   *Gen. 17:1-14*

Promise of a true son   *Gen. 15:4; 18:9-15*
Fulfillment of the promise   *Gen. 21:1-7*

Absalom
David's son   *2 Sam. 3:3*
Conspired against David   *2 Sam. 15:1-12*
David fled from   *2 Sam. 15:13-17*
Killed by Joab   *2 Sam. 18:9-17*
Mourned by David   *2 Sam. 18:33*

Abstinence from Alcohol (See also
   Drinking, Drunkenness, Wine)
By Israel's priests   *Lev. 10:8-11*
By Nazirites   *Num. 6:3-4*
Wisdom of   *Prov. 23:20-21, 29-35*
For a weaker brother's sake   *Rom. 14:13-21*
By deacons and elders   *1 Tim. 3:2-3, 8; Titus 1:7*

Abundance (See also Blessing, Money, Riches)
God's blessing on the obedient   *Deut. 30:9-10*
Subject to God's judgment   *Luke 12:13-21*
■ Characteristic of:
   God's character   *Exod. 34:6-7*
   God's grace   *Rom. 5:17, 20; 1 Tim. 1:14*
   Christian life   *John 10:10*

Accusation, False (See also Lying,
   Persecution)
Condemned by God   *Exod. 20:16; 23:1, 7; Lev. 19:16*
Characteristic of Satan   *Rev. 12:9-10*

Achan
Responsible for Israelites' rout at Ai   *Josh. 7:1-23*
Stoned   *Josh. 7:24-26*

Achish
King of Gath   *1 Sam. 21:10*
David feigns insanity in front of   *1 Sam. 21:1-15*

Acting Wisely (See also Behavior, Prudence, Wisdom)
Example of David   *1 Sam. 18:5, 14-15, 30*
Part of godly character   *Ps. 101:2*

Adam (See also Eve, Fall of Man)
The first man   *Gen. 1:26-2:8*
His sin and punishment   *Gen. 2:8-3:24*
His role and Christ's compared   *Rom. 5:12-21*

Admonishment (See also Chastisement, Counsel)
■ Duty of:
Fathers   *Eph. 6:4*
Spiritual leaders   *1 Thess. 5:12*
All Christians   *Rom. 15:14*
■ Sources of:
Scripture   *1 Cor. 10:11*
Wise men   *Eccles. 12:11-12*
Spiritual knowledge   *Col. 3:16*

Adolescence (See also Youth)
■ Instruction for:
A wise son   *Prov. 13:1*
All youth   *Prov. 23:22*
Ridicule in   *Job 30:1*
Mockery in   *Prov. 30:17*
Cursing in   *Prov. 20:20*
Running away from lusts in   *2 Tim. 2:22*
Rejoicing in   *Eccles. 11:9*
Remembering the Creator in   *Eccles. 12:1*
Not to be despised   *1 Tim. 4:12*

Adonijah
Fourth son of David   *1 Kings 1:5, 11, 25*
Pardoned by Solomon   *1 Kings 1:53*

Adoption, Literal and Spiritual (See also
    Family, Fatherhood, Orphan)
Israel adopted by God   *Deut. 14:1–2*
Gentiles adopted by God   *Eph. 3:1–6*
Through the Spirit   *Rom. 8:14–17, 23*
Predestined   *Rom. 8:29–30*
Through belief in Christ   *John 1:12–13*
Object of Christ's mission   *Gal. 4:4–5*

Adultery (See also Fornication, Lust)
Forbidden by God   *Exod. 20:14; Deut. 5:18*
Defined by Christ   *Matt. 5:27–28, 32*
Deserves God's judgment   *Heb. 13:4*
Symbolic of Israel's sin   *Ezek. 16:1–63; Hos. 1:2*
Symbolic of worldliness   *James 4:1–5; Rev. 17:1–6*

Adversity (See also Affliction, Pain, Trouble)
■ Caused by:
   Man's sin   *Gen. 3:16–17; Lev. 26:14–39*
   God's discipline   *Heb. 12:5–11*
■ In order to:
   Punish for sin   *1 Sam. 12:9–12*
   Teach dependence upon God   *Deut. 8:2–6*
   Purify our faith   *2 Pet. 1:5–8*
   Produce strong character   *James 1:2–3*

Aeneas
Healing of   *Acts 9:33*

Affection (See also Friendship, Love)
Christ claims first place   *Matt. 10:37*
Paul modelling Christ's   *Phil. 1:8*

■ To be shown by:
Spouses to each other   *Eph. 5:21–33; Titus 2:4*
All Christians to one another   *Rom. 12:10*

Affliction (See also Adversity, Pain, Suffering)
Of the righteous   *Amos 5:12; Heb. 11:35–38*
To teach obedience   *Ps. 119:67; Job 5:6–7, 17–18*
To test faith   *Mark 4:17*
Cannot separate believer from God   *Rom. 8:35–39*
To be ended by Christ   *1 Thess. 1:4–7*

Agabus
Foretold famine and suffering   *Acts 11:28; 21:10*

Agriculture (See also Farming, Vine)
Established by God's direction   *Gen. 2:15*
Related to the rhythm of creation   *Gen. 8:22*
Image of God's Word   *Isa. 55:10–11*
Parables related to   *Matt. 13:1–43*
God's providence in   *Matt. 5:45; 2 Cor. 9:10–12*

Agrippa
Paul's defense before   *Acts 25:22–26:32*

Ahasuerus, Xerxes (See also Esther, Haman, Mordecai)
Made Esther queen   *Esther 1:1; 2:17*
His decree to destroy Jews   *Esther 3:12*
Hanged Haman   *Esther 7:9; 8:7*
Advanced Mordecai   *Esther 9:4*

Ahaziah
Wicked reign as king of Judah   *2 Kings 8:25*
As king of Israel   *1 Kings 22:40, 49*
Injury, idolatry, judgment, and death   *2 Kings 1:1–17*

Ahimelech
Helped David   *1 Sam. 21:1–6*

Ahithophel
His counsel esteemed   *2 Sam. 16:23*
His advice to Absalom   *2 Sam. 17:1–4*
His suicide   *2 Sam. 17:23*

Allegory (See also Symbol)
Of Israel's unfaithfulness   *Ezek. 16:1–17:24*
Of Christ as shepherd   *John 10:1–29*
Of the Old and New Covenants   *Gal. 4:21–31*
Of Israel and the Gentiles   *Rom. 11:13–24*
Of the Christian's armor   *Eph. 6:10–18*

Alliance (See also Diplomacy, Politics)
Forbidden with idolaters   *Exod. 23:32–33; 34:11–16*
Forbidden with unbelievers   *2 Kings 23:31–25:21*
Example of disobedience and punishment   *2 Cor. 6:14*

Altar (See also Offering, Sacrifice)
Earliest example   *Gen. 8:20*
Of incense   *Exod. 27:1–8; 30:1–10*
Jordan memorial   *Deut. 27:1–8*
Of Jeroboam at Bethel   *1 Kings 12:32–33*
Of Ezekiel's vision (burnt offering)   *Ezek. 43:13–27*
Of John's vision (incense)   *Rev. 8:3–4*

Altruism (See also Kindness, Love, Selfishness)
■ Manifested in:
Service   *Matt. 20:26–28*
Seeking another's welfare   *Phil. 2:3–4*
Helping the weak   *Acts 20:35; Rom. 15:1–3*
■ Examples:
Moses   *Exod. 32:30–34*
Jesus   *John 13:1–20; Phil. 2:5–8*
Paul   *1 Cor. 9:19–23*

Amasa
Absalom's captain   *2 Sam. 17:25*

Amaziah

Godly reign as king of Judah   *2 Kings 14:1*
Defeated by Joash, king of Israel   *2 Chron. 25:21*

Ambassador (See also Alliance, Diplomacy, Politics)

- Representative to:
  Obtain favor   *Num. 20:14–21; 2 Kings 16:7*
  Settle disputes   *Judg. 11:12–28*
  Issue an ultimatum   *2 Kings 19:9–14*
  Ask God's blessing   *Jer. 37:3*
- Symbolic of:
  Christ's servants   *2 Cor. 5:20*
  Paul in particular   *Eph. 6:20*

Ambition (See also Presumption, Pride, Self-will)

Evil, example of Babel   *Gen. 11:1–9*
- Evil, inspired by:
  Satan   *Gen. 3:1–6; Luke 4:5–8*
  Pride   *Isa. 14:12–15; 1 Tim. 3:6*
  Jealousy   *Num. 12:1–2*
- Godly:
  For the best gifts   *1 Cor. 12:31*
  For holiness   *Phil. 3:12–14*
  For the spread of the gospel   *Rom. 15:20*

Amen

- Used in Old Testament to:
  Express agreement   *Num. 5:22*
  Affirm a doxology   *1 Chron. 16:36*
  Confirm an oath   *Neh. 5:13*
- In the New Testament:
  Emphatic closing to benedictions   *Rom. 15:33; 16:25–27*
  Emphasized the truth of a statement   *John 3:3, 5, 11*
  Uttered through Christ   *2 Cor. 1:20*

Amusement (See also Games, Pleasure)
The futility of   *Eccles. 7:2–6*
Example of Moses' renunciation of   *Heb. 11:25*
May lead to rejection of God   *Job 21:12–16*
May lead to spiritual death   *Luke 8:14; 1 Tim. 5:6*
Pursuing this indicates sinfulness   *1 Pet. 4:3–5*
Part of the rejection of God's prophets   *Rev. 11:10*

Ananias
(and Sapphira) Their lie and death   *Acts 5:1*
The disciple, sent to Paul   *Acts 9:10*
The high priest, Paul brought before   *Acts 22:30*

Anarchy (See also Government, Society)
■ Typical of:
  Israel before the kingdom   *Judg. 17:6; 18:1–31*
  The condition of Israel under judgment   *Isa. 3:5–8*
  The day of antichrist   *2 Thess. 2:3–12*
■ Demonstrated by:
  Rampant immorality   *Exod. 32:1–8, 25*
  Unchecked injustice and violence   *Hab. 1:1–4*
  Spiritual confusion and idolatry   *Judg. 17:1–13*

Ancestors (See also Family, Genealogy)
God's faithfulness to them   *Lev. 26:45*
Character perpetuated in descendants   *Jer. 11:10*

Anchor, Spiritual (See also Hope)
Of the soul   *Heb. 6:19*

Ammon
Children of   *Gen. 19:38*
Prophecies concerning nation   *Jer. 25:21*

Amnon
Son of David   *2 Sam. 3:2*
Raped half-sister Tamar   *2 Sam. 13:1–22*

Amos
Shepherd called to prophesy   *Amos 1:1; 7:14*
Told by priest not to prophesy   *Amos 7:16*
Saw vision depicting Israel's end   *Amos 8:1–2*

Ancient of Days (See also God)
Title applied to God the Father   *Dan. 7:9, 13, 22*

Andrew
One of the apostles   *Matt. 10:2; Acts 1:13*

Angels (See also Cherubim, Gabriel, Michael, Seraphim)
Spiritual servants of God   *Heb. 1:14*
Heralds of Christ   *Matt. 1:20–21; 28:5–7; Luke 2:10–12; Acts 1:9–11*
■ Ministry to believers:
Guidance   *Gen. 24:7, 40; Acts 8:26*
Provision for needs   *1 Kings 19:5–8*
Protection and deliverance   *Ps. 34:7*
Comfort   *Acts 27:23–24*
■ Ministry to unbelievers:
Destruction   *Gen. 19:13*
Cursing   *Judg. 5:23*
Sudden death   *Acts 12:23*
Execution of judgment   *Matt. 13:41–42, 49–50*

Anger (See also Hatred, Wrath)
Evil   *Gen. 4:6; 49:7; Ps. 37:8; Prov. 22:24; Matt. 5:22*
God's, over sin   *Num. 32:10–15*
Christ's   *Mark 3:5*
Must be dealt with   *Eph. 4:26–27*

Animals (See also Birds, Offering, Sacrifice)
Clean and unclean   *Lev. 11:1–31; Acts 10:9–15*
For sacrifices   *Lev. 5:6–10; 16:3–5; Exod. 12:3–6*
Symbolic of world empires   *Dan. 7:2–8*

Anna
Prophetess who finally saw Messiah   Luke 2:36

Annas
High priest who judged Christ   John 18:13, 24
Peter and John brought before him   Acts 4:6

Anointed One, (See also Messiah)
Foreshadowed in the Old Testament   Isa. 61:1
Confirmed in Christ   Matt. 16:16, 20; Luke 4:18–19;
    Acts 4:26–27; 9:22; Heb. 1:9

Anointing (See also Dedication, Oil)
Symbolizes sanctification   Exod. 30:22–32
■ Physical, performed upon:
Priests   Exod. 29:7
Prophets   1 Kings 19:16
Kings   1 Sam. 10:1; 1 Kings 19:15–16
■ Spiritual, by the Holy Spirit:
Predicted by Joel   Joel 2:28–29
Predicted by Christ   John 7:38–39
Received at Pentecost   Acts 2:1–4
Received at conversion   John 2:20, 27; 1 Cor. 12:13

Anthropomorphism
■ Physical examples:
Feet and hands   Exod. 24:10–11
Mouth   Num. 12:8
Eyes   Hab. 1:13; 1 Pet. 3:12
■ Non-physical examples:
Change of mind   Gen. 6:6; Exod. 32:14
Consideration of a matter   Gen. 18:17–21
Memory   Gen. 9:6; Exod. 2:24

Antichrist
Coming predicted   2 Thess. 2:3–12; 1 John 2:18;
    Rev. 11:7

Characteristic attitude: denying God   *2 Thess. 2:3–4*
Deceiver of the world   *2 John 7; Rev. 19:20*
Persecutor of Christians   *Rev. 13:7*
Epitome of general sin   *2 Thess. 2:3, 7*
To be destroyed at Christ's return   *2 Thess. 2:8;
    Rev. 19:20*

Anxiety (See also Care, Stress, Worry)
Characteristic of a godless life   *Matt. 6:31–32*
■ Overcome by:
  Putting God's will first   *Matt. 6:33*
  A realistic perspective on life   *Matt. 6:34*
  Trust in the Lord   *Ps. 37:1–7*
  Reliance upon the Holy Spirit   *Mark 13:11*
  Confidence in God   *Rom. 8:28–39*
  Commitment to God   *Phil. 4:6–7; 1 Pet. 5:6–7*

Apollos
Eloquent in the Scriptures   *Acts 18:24; 19:1*

Apostasy (See also Backsliding, Heresy, Idolatry)
Of an individual   *1 Sam. 15:11; Heb. 3:12*
Of a nation   *1 Kings 12:25–33*
Of angels   *2 Pet. 2:4; Rev. 12:7–9*
Punishment is certain   *Heb. 10:26–29*
■ Caused by:
  Evil influences   *Matt. 13:20–21; Acts 20:29–30*
  Evil desires   *2 Tim. 4:3–4*
  Spiritual disease   *Acts 28:25–27*

Apostle (See also Disciple, Witness)
Title of Jesus   *Heb. 3:1*
Designation of the Twelve   *Luke 6:13–16*
Listing of the Twelve   *Matt. 10:2–4*
■ Appointed to:
  Preach the gospel   *Matt. 28:19–20; Acts 1:8*
  Write Scripture   *Eph. 3:4–5*
  Establish the church   *Eph. 2:20*

Apparel (See also Clothing)
■ Symbolizes:
God's judgment   *Isa. 63:1-3*
God's selection of his people   *Ezek. 16:8-14*
God's redemption   *Zech. 3:1-7*
The church's purity   *Rev. 19:7-8*

Appearance
■ Of Christ:
On the cross   *Isa. 52:14; 53:7*
At the transfiguration   *Matt. 17:2*
At the grave of Lazarus   *John 11:38*
Of his hands and side   *John 20:20, 27*

Aquila
Husband of Priscilla   *Acts 18:2*
Tentmaker driven out of Rome   *Acts 18:2*
Went with Paul to Ephesus   *Acts 18:19*
Commended   *Rom. 16:3; 1 Cor. 16:19*

Argument (See also Quarrel, Strife)
Forbidden in secondary matters   *Rom. 14:1*
Used by Paul in his evangelism   *Acts 9:29; 17:17; 19:8-9*
Characteristic of evil men   *1 Tim. 6:4-5*
Example of Job's   *Job 23:1-7*

Ark (See also Ark of the Covenant)
Noah's   *Gen. 6:5-8:19; 1 Pet. 3:20-21*

Ark of the Covenant (See also Tabernacle)
Description   *Exod. 25:10-22*
Expression of God's holiness   *Lev. 16:2-3; 1 Sam. 6:19-20; 2 Sam 6:6-7*
Place of atonement   *Lev. 16:2, 13-17; Heb. 9:1-10*
Type of Christ   *Heb. 9:11-14*

Arm of God (See also Anthropomorphism)

■ As a symbol of God's power in:
Creation   *Jer. 27:5; 32:17*
The Exodus   *Exod. 6:6; 15:16; Deut. 11:2*
Preserving his people   *Deut. 33:27*
Judgment   *Ps. 89:10, 13; Jer. 21:5*
Redemption   *Isa. 40:10–11*

Armageddon

Site of end-time battle   *Rev. 16:16*

Armor (See also War, Weapon)

■ As symbol:
Of Christian character   *Rom. 13:12*
Of spiritual resources   *Eph. 6:11–17*
Goliath's and Saul's   *1 Sam. 17:5–7, 38–39*

Army (See also War)

Israel's first   *Josh. 5:13–6:5*
Symbolic of the church   *Eph. 6:12; 2 Cor. 10:3–6*
End-time armies   *Dan. 11:7–45; 19:19*

Arrest

Of Jesus in Gethsemane   *Matt. 26:50; Mark 14:46*
Of apostles after Pentecost   *Acts 5:17–18; 6:12*
Of Paul and Silas   *Acts 16:19*
Of Paul   *Acts 21:30–33*

Arrogance (See also Boasting, Conceit, Pride)

Condemned   *1 Sam. 2:3*
Hated by God   *Prov. 8:13*
To be judged by God   *Isa. 13:11*
Crucial sin of Moab   *Jer. 48:29*

Art (See also Creativity)

Early development   *Gen. 4:21–22*
Expression of service to God   *Exod. 31:1–11*

Ascension (See also Resurrection)

Of Enoch   *Gen. 5:24; Heb. 11:5*
Of Elijah   *2 Kings 2:11*
Of Jesus Christ   *Mark 16:19; Luke 24:50; Acts 1:9-11*
Beginning of Christ's exaltation   *Acts 2:32-36*

Asceticism (See also Abstinence from alcohol, Celibacy, Fasting)

Old Testament examples   *Num. 6:1-21*
Characteristic of John the Baptist   *Matt. 3:4; 11:18*
Rebuked by Paul   *Col. 2:20-23; 1 Tim. 4:1-5*
Positive teaching   *1 Cor. 9:24-27; 2 Tim. 2:3-5*

Asherah, Asherim

Images of Canaanite religion   *Deut. 6:5*
Removed by Asa   *2 Chron. 14:5*
Removed by Jehoshaphat   *2 Chron. 17:6*
Worshiped by Judah   *2 Chron. 24:17-18*

Ashes (See also Mourning, Sorrow)

- Symbolic of:
  Purification   *Num. 19:17-19; Heb. 9:13*
  Mourning   *2 Sam. 13:19; Esth. 4:1, 3; Isa. 61:3*
  Repentance   *Job 42:6; Matt. 11:21*
  Humility before God   *Dan. 9:3*

Asa

Godly king of Judah   *1 Kings 15:9, 11*
Wrongly sought aid of Syrians   *2 Chron. 16:1-10*
Death of   *2 Chron. 16:11-14*

Asahel

Killed by Abner in self-defense   *2 Sam. 2:18-23*

Asher

Son of Jacob   *Gen. 30:13*
Inheritance in Promised Land   *Josh. 19:24*

Ashtaroth
Goddess of Canaanites   *Josh. 9:10*
- Idolatrous worship of:
  By Israel   *Judg. 2:13; 1 Sam. 12:10*
  By Solomon   *1 Kings 11:5, 33*

Assault and Battery (See also Beating)
Old Testament laws   *Exod. 21:15, 18–19*
Jesus' comments   *Matt. 5:38–39*
Jesus as victim   *Matt. 26:67; 27:30; Mark 14:65*

Assembly (See also Church)
- Term for:
  Israel as a nation   *Judg. 20:2; 2 Chron. 30:23*
  God's elect people   *Ps. 111:1*
  A community meeting   *Acts 19:32, 39, 41*
  A local church   *James 2:2*
  The heavenly church   *Heb. 12:23*

Assurance (See also Confidence, Hope)
Rooted in faith   *Eph. 3:20; 2 Tim. 1:12; Heb. 10:22*
Expressed in hope   *Heb. 6:11, 19*
Confirmed by love   *John 3:14, 18–19; 4:18*
Resting in God's power   *John 10:28–30*
Sealed by Christ's work   *Rom. 8:28–39*
Witnessed to by the Spirit   *Rom. 8:15–16*

Astrology (See also Magic, Star, Witchcraft)
Vain hope   *Isa. 47:12–15*
Vain help   *Dan. 5:7–8*
Vanity, compared with God   *Dan. 2:27–28*

Astronomy (See also Star)
Guide to God's handiwork   *Gen. 1:3–8; Job 38:31–33; Ps. 8:3; 19:1–6; Amos 5:8*
Stars as symbol of Israel   *Gen. 15:5; Jer. 31:35–37; 33:22*

Athaliah
Daughter of Ahab, mother of Ahaziah   2 Kings 8:26
Killed royal family   2 Kings 11:1; 2 Chron. 22:10
Killed by order of Jehoiada   2 Kings 11:16

Atheism (See also Apostasy)
Characteristic of the wicked   Ps. 10:4; Rom. 1:20-32
Characteristic of the fool   Ps. 14:1; 53:1
Example of Pharaoh   Exod. 5:2

Atonement (See also Atonement, Day of; Justification, Propitiation)
Sin offering ritual   Lev. 16:1-34
Accepted by God for forgiveness   Lev. 5:10-13
Work of Christ   Rom. 3:22-25; Heb. 9:11-14

Atonement, Day of
Time specified   Lev. 16:29-31, 34; 23:27
Ritual specified   Lev. 16:1-34; 23:26-32
Type of Christ's sacrifice   Heb. 9:11-14

Attributes of God (See God)

Authority (See also Ruler, Sovereignty)
Jesus taught with   Matt. 7:29
To forgive sin   Matt. 9:6
To cast out demons   Mark 3:15
In heaven and on earth   Matt. 28:18
None, except from God   Rom. 13:1
Submit to   Titus 3:1

Avarice (See also Covetousness, Greed)
An example of vain desire   Eccles. 4:7-8; 5:10-11
Not characteristic of a Christian elder   1 Tim. 3:2
Produces grief   1 Tim. 6:9-10
Once led to national crisis   Josh. 7:1-26
Once led to an innocent's death   1 Kings 21:1-14

Avenger of Blood

First description   *Gen. 9:5*
Mosaic laws   *Num. 35:19–29; Deut. 19:4–13*
Laws restated   *Josh. 20:1–9*
Law set aside by David   *2 Sam. 14:4–14*

Awe (See also Fear, Reverence)

Proper reaction to God   *Ps. 33:8*
Proper reaction to God's Word   *Ps. 119:161*

B

Baal (See also Idolatry)
Pagan male deity   *Judg. 10:6; 1 Sam. 7:4*
- Worship of:
  Involved immorality   *Num. 25:1–5; Hos. 9:10*
  Involved idolatry and atrocities   *1 Kings 19:18*
  Introduced to Israel by Ahab   *1 Kings 16:30–32*
  Elijah's triumph over   *1 Kings 18:17–40*
  Denounced by Jeremiah   *Jer. 2:8, 23; 7:9*

Babel (See also Babylon)
Story of its famous tower   *Gen. 11:1–9*

Baby (See also Children)
Declare God's glory   *Ps. 8:2*
Description of new believer   *1 Pet. 2:2*
Symbol of immaturity   *1 Cor. 3:1–2; Heb. 5:13*

Babylon (See also Babel, Nebuchadnezzar)
Mighty, ancient kingdom   *Dan. 4:30; Isa. 13:19; 14:4*
Conqueror of Jerusalem   *2 Chron. 36:17–21*
Destruction predicted   *Isa. 13:1–22; Jer. 50:1–46*
Symbol of evil society   *Rev. 17:1–18:24*

Backbiting (See also Gossip, Slander)
Not characteristic of godly   *Ps. 15:1–3; 1 Pet. 2:1*
Characteristic of evil   *Rom. 1:18, 30; 2 Cor. 12:20*
Produces angry response   *Prov. 25:23*
Will be judged   *Ps. 101:5*

Backsliding (See also Apostacy)
Early warnings against   *Lev. 26:14–42; Deut. 4:9; 8:11*
Demonstrated in parable   *Mark 4:7, 15–19*
Christ's warnings   *Luke 9:62; John 15:6*
Paul recounts Israel's   *1 Cor. 10:1–13*
To be repented of   *Rev. 2:4–5; 3:2–3*

Bad Company (See also Worldliness)
Contagious sin   Num. 16:26
Avoided by good men   Ps. 1:1; 26:4-5
Compared with God's company   Ps. 84:10
To be shunned   Prov. 1:10-19; Rom. 16:17-18
Partnership with, forbidden   2 Cor. 6:14-16

Balaam
Story of   Num. 22:1-24:25; 31:8
Symbol of evil teachers   2 Pet. 2:15; Jude 11; Rev. 2:14

Banishment
Adam and Eve from Eden   Gen. 3:22-24
Cain   Gen. 4:12-14
Israel into exile   2 Chron. 36:20-21
The Jews from Rome   Acts 18:2
Satan from heaven   Rev. 12:7-9
The wicked to hell   Rev. 20:15; 21:8

Baptism (See also John the Baptist)
By John the Baptist   Matt. 3:5-12
Jesus' baptism   Matt. 3:11, 13-17
Commanded by Christ   Matt. 28:19-20
■ By the Holy Spirit:
  Predicted by prophets   Joel 2:28-29
  Predicted by Christ   Acts 1:5
  At Pentecost   Acts 2:16-21
In the early church   Acts 8:12, 36-38; 9:17-18

Barabbas
Exchanged for Christ before Pilate   Matt. 27:16-26
Referred to by Peter   Acts 3:14

Barnabas
Early example of sharing   Acts 4:36-37
Supporter of Paul   Acts 9:27; 11:22-26; 13:1-14:28
Addressed Jerusalem council   Acts 15:1-35

Separation from Paul   *Acts 15:36-40*
Paul's testimony about   *1 Cor. 9:6; Gal. 2:1, 9, 13*

Barrenness (See also Sterility)
A reproach   *Gen. 16:2; 30:22-23*
A judgment   *2 Sam. 6:23*
The absence of God's blessing   *Exod. 23:26*
Removed by God   *Ps. 113:9*
Jesus' response to a fig tree   *Mark 11:12-14, 20-22*
Defense against spiritual   *2 Pet. 1:5-8*

Bartholomew
One of the apostles   *Matt. 10:3; Acts 1:13*

Bartimaeus
Blind beggar healed by Jesus   *Mark 10:46-52*

Bathing (See also Washing)
Of Pharaoh's daughter   *Exod. 2:5*
Of Bathsheba   *2 Sam. 11:2*
For refreshment of feet   *Gen. 24:32; John 13:10*
For ceremonial cleansing   *Lev. 14:8; 2 Kings 5:10-14*
As part of Jewish rituals   *Mark 7:2*

Bathsheba
Relationship with David   *2 Sam 11:1-27*
Children born to   *2 Sam. 12:14-19, 24; 1 Chron. 3:5*
Secures throne for Solomon   *1 Kings 1:11-31*
Adonijah's dealings with   *1 Kings 2:13-25*

Battle (See also Army, War)
Gideon against the Midianites   *Judg. 7:20-21*
Involving priests   *2 Chron. 13:12*
Prayer preceding it   *2 Chron. 14:11; 20:3-12*

Beard (See also Hair)
Long, worn by leaders   *Ps. 133:2; Judg. 16:17*
Sign of holiness   *Lev. 19:27; 21:5*

Beating (See also Assault and Battery)
For the disobedient   *Luke 12:47–48*
Unjust, of a servant   *Luke 20:10–11*
Of Christ   *Isa. 50:6; Mark 15:19*
Of the apostles   *Acts 5:40*
Of Paul   *Acts 16:19–24*

Beauty (See also Art)
Vanity of it   *Prov. 31:30*
Danger of it   *Prov. 6:25–29; 2 Sam. 11:2–5*
■ Symbolized:
  God's care   *Hos. 14:6; Matt. 6:28–29*
  In the Messiah and his bride   *Ps. 45:2–3, 8, 11–14*
  In Zion   *Ps. 50:2*
  In the feet of preachers   *Isa. 52:7; Rom. 10:15*

Beelzebub
Prince of devils   *Matt. 12:24; Mark 3:22*

Beggar (See also Poverty)
Not the fate of the righteous   *Ps. 37:25*
Cursed state   *Ps. 109:8–11*
Christ's contact with   *Mark 10:46–52*
Parable of Lazarus   *Luke 16:19–31*
Peter's and John's healing of   *Acts 3:1–10*

Behavior (See also Conduct, Morality)
Toward neighbor   *Matt. 7:12; Rom. 15:2*
In accord with Christ   *Rom. 15:5*
That glorifies God   *Rom. 15:6*
Toward enemies   *Matt. 5:39–42*

Belief (See also Confidence, Faith, Unbelief)
Godly response   *Gen. 15:6; John 1:7, 12; 3:16*
Results in victory   *2 Chron. 20:20–30; Mark 9:17–27*
Integral to Jesus' preaching   *Mark 1:15; 11:22–24*

Part of early confession   *Rom. 10:9*
Mark of the true Christian   *1 John 5:13*

Believer (See Belief, Christian, Disciple)

Belshazzar
Writing on the wall   *Dan. 5:1-6*
His judgment by Daniel, his death   *Dan. 5:13-30*

Benediction
Earliest example   *Gen. 1:22, 28*
Pronounced upon Abraham   *Gen. 14:19-20*
By Jacob upon his sons   *Gen. 48:15–49:28*
Priestly, instituted by God   *Deut. 10:8; 21:5*
Aaronic   *Num. 6:23-26*
Mosaic   *Deut. 33:1-29*
Pronounced upon Jesus   *Luke 2:34-35*
Pronounced by Jesus   *Luke 24:50*
Pronounced by the apostles   *Rom. 15:5-6, 13*

Beneficence (See also Benevolence, Generosity, Liberality, Kindness)
Ordained by the Law   *Deut. 15:7-15, 18*
Blessing upon those who give   *Ps. 41:1; Prov. 22:9*
Characteristic of God   *Ps. 112:9*
Ordained by Christ   *Matt. 5:42; 25:35-45; Mark 9:41*
In the early church   *Acts 6:1-6; 2 Cor. 8:1-6*
Rewarded in heaven   *1 Tim. 6:17-19*
Lack of, cursed   *Prov. 28:27; 1 Tim. 5:8; 1 John 3:17*

Benevolence (See also Charity, Love)
Toward the poor and needy   *Gal. 2:10; Eph. 4:28*
Towards enemies   *Prov. 25:21-22; Matt. 5:39, 43-44*
Useless if not motivated by love   *1 Cor. 13:3*
Worth of is relative to giver   *Mark 12:41-44*
Part of Christian responsibility   *Rom. 12:13*
A sacrifice pleasing to God   *Heb. 13:16*
Brings blessing   *Prov. 11:25; Isa. 58:10-11; Acts 20:35*

Ben-Hadad

King of Assyria allied with Asa   *1 Kings 15:18*
Baffled by Elisha   *2 Kings 6:8*
Besieged Samaria   *2 Kings 6:24*
Killed by Hazael   *2 Kings 8:7*

Benjamin

- Individual:
  His birth   *Gen. 35:16–18*
  His visit to Egypt   *Gen. 43:1–45:15*
- The tribe:
  Prophecies about   *Gen. 49:27; Deut. 33:12*
  Scandal, war, and renewal   *Judg. 19:1–21:23*
  Famous people from   *1 Sam. 9:1–2; Phil. 3:5*

Bereavement (See also Death, Grief, Mourning)

- Examples of accompanying emotions:
  Sorrow   *Gen. 37:34–35; Exod. 12:29–30*
  Deep feeling   *2 Sam. 18:33*
  Bitterness   *Ruth 1:20–21*
- Godly responses:
  Submission   *Job 1:20–22*
  Hope   *John 11:21–27; 1 Thess. 4:13–18*
  Sorrow   *John 11:35; Acts 9:39*

Bethany

Location   *Luke 19:29; John 11:18*
Home of Mary, Martha and Lazarus   *John 11:1*
Scene of the Ascension   *Luke 24:50–51*

Bethel

Jacob dreamed there and named it   *Gen. 28:10–19*
Renewal of Jacob's covenant there   *Gen. 35:1–15*

Bethlehem

Place of Messiah's birth   *Mic. 5:2; Matt. 2:1, 5*
Where infants were killed   *Jer. 31:15; Matt. 2:16*

Betrayal (See also Treason)
Of Samson by Delilah   *Judg. 16:15-20*
Of Abner by Joab   *2 Sam. 3:26-27*
■ Of Christ:
   Predicted   *Ps. 41:9; Matt. 17:22*
   Betrayer identified   *John 13:21-30*
   In Gethsemane   *Matt. 26:14-15, 47-50*
Guilt of Judas   *Matt. 27:3-8*

Betrothal (See also Marriage)
Of Jacob   *Gen. 29:18-30*
Of Mary and Joseph   *Matt. 1:18; Luke 1:27*
■ Figurative of:
   Israel's relationship to God   *Hos. 2:19-20*
   Church's relationship to Christ   *2 Cor. 11:2*

Bigotry (See also Racism, Tolerance)
■ Examples of:
   Haman toward Jews   *Esther 3:1-11*
   Jews toward Samaritans   *John 4:9*
   Jews toward Christians   *1 Thess. 2:14-16*
   Jews toward Gentiles   *Acts 10:28*
   Among believers   *Gal. 2:11-14*

Bildad
Friend of Job   *Job 2:11*
His answers to Job   *Job 8; 18; 25*

Birds (See also Animals)
Created and sustained by God   *Gen. 1:20-21*
Sent by divine providence   *Exod. 16:12-31*
Used in sacrifices   *Lev. 1:14; Luke 2:24*

Birth (See also Baby, Incarnation, Motherhood)
■ Of Jesus:
   Foretold; fulfilled   *Mic. 5:2; Matt. 1:18*
New   *John 3:3-8; 1 Pet. 1:23*

Birthright (See also Firstborn, Heir, Inheritance)
- Lost:
  By Esau to Jacob   *Gen. 25:29–34; 27:6–40*
  By Reuben because of sin   *Gen. 49:3–4*
  By Manasseh to Ephraim   *Gen. 48:15–20*

Bishop (See also Elder)
Qualifications   *1 Tim. 3:1–7; Titus 1:6–9*
Duties   *Acts 20:17, 28–30*
Responsibilities   *1 Thess. 5:14; Heb. 13:17*
Exhortation to, by Peter   *1 Pet. 5:1–3*

Bitterness (See also Anger, Retaliation)
Of water   *Exod. 15:23–25*
Of Passover herbs   *Exod. 12:8; Num. 9:11*
A result of sin   *Prov. 5:4; Acts 8:23*
- To be avoided:
  In personal relationships   *Eph. 4:31; Col. 3:21*
  As sin   *Heb. 12:15; James 3:14*

Blasphemy (See also Profanity, Swearing)
- Forbidden by God:
  The Law   *Exod. 20:7; Lev. 19:12; Deut. 5:11*
  Example of punishment   *Lev. 24:10–16*
  Against the Holy Spirit   *Matt. 12:31–32; Luke 12:10*

Blessedness (See also Happiness, Joy)
- Condition of those who:
  Are forgiven by God   *Ps. 32:1–2*
  Are disciplined by God   *Ps. 94:12*
  Identify with God   *Matt. 5:3–12*
  Are chosen in Christ   *Eph. 1:3–4*
  Believe   *Gal. 3:9*
  Are justified   *Rom. 4:5–9*

Blessing (See also Abundance, Reward)
Result of obedience   *Deut. 28:1–2*

Comes from God   *Prov. 3:1-2; James 1:17*
Physical   *Deut. 28:1-14*
Of Israelites   *Rom. 9:4-5*
Spiritual   *Ps. 23; Isa. 40:11, 29, 31; Rom. 8:1-2, 26-39*

Blindness (See also Darkness)

Sent by God as judgment   *Gen. 19:11; Deut. 28:28*
Healed by Jesus   *Matt. 9:27-30; 20:30-34*
Spiritual   *Prov. 4:19; Matt. 6:23*
■ Spiritual condition of:
    Jewish leaders   *Matt. 15:14; 23:19, 24, 26*
    Israel   *2 Cor. 3:14-16*
    Unbelievers and the disobedient   *2 Cor. 4:3-4*

Blood (See also Atonement, Offering, Sacrifice)

Symbolizes life   *Gen. 9:4-6; Lev. 17:11, 14; Matt. 27:24*
Forbidden as food   *Gen. 9:4; Lev. 3:17*
Importance in sacrificial system   *Heb. 9:22*
Plague upon Egypt   *Exod. 7:17-24*
■ Christ's:
    Atonement, propitiation   *Heb. 9:12-14, 18-28*
    Symbolized in the wine   *Matt. 26:28*
    Operative today   *1 John 1:7; Rev. 12:11*

Boasting (See also Arrogance, Conceit, Pride)

Proper, in God   *Ps. 34:2; 2 Cor. 10:13-17*
■ Vain, because of:
    The uncertainty of life   *Prov. 27:1*
    The sovereignty of God   *Luke 12:16-21*
    Salvation by grace   *Eph. 2:8-9*

Boaz

Conduct toward Ruth   *Ruth 2-4*
Ancestor of David and Christ   *Matt. 1:5; Luke 3:23, 32*

Body

Made by God   *Gen. 2:7, 21-22; Ps. 139:13-14*
Subject to death   *Rom. 5:12*

■ Christ's:
Formed by God   *Luke 1:34–35*
Like ours   *Heb. 2:14; 4:15*
Resurrected without corruption   *Acts 2:31*
Symbolized in the bread   *Mark 14:22*
Descriptive of the church   *Eph. 1:22–23; Col. 1:24*

Boldness (See also Confidence, Courage)
The result of faith in God   *Prov. 14:26; 28:1*
Given through Christ   *Eph. 3:12; Heb. 4:15–16*
■ Should be characteristic of:
Fellowship with God   *Heb. 10:19–22*
Preaching   *Acts 9:27–29; Eph. 6:19; Phil. 1:14*
Christian hope   *1 John 2:28; 4:17*

Bondage (See also Captivity, Liberty, Servant)
Israel in Egypt   *Exod. 1:7–22; 2:23; 6:6*
Israel in Assyria   *2 Kings 17:6, 20–23*
Judah in Babylon   *2 Kings 25:8–12*
An individual in Israel   *Lev. 25:39–43*
■ Figurative of:
Sinful condition   *John 8:34; Rom. 6:6–17*
Submission to the Law   *Gal. 4:21–5:1*
Devotion to Christ   *Rom. 1:1; 6:18, 22; Phil. 1:1*

Book
Characteristics of ancient   *Jer. 36:2; 2 Tim. 4:13*
■ Of the Law:
Foundation of Israel's religion   *Deut. 28:58*
Lost and found   *2 Kings 22:8*
Brought renewal   *2 Kings 23:2–14; Neh. 8:2–3, 8–18*
■ Of Life:
Contents   *Mal. 3:16–18; Phil. 4:3; Rev. 13:8; 17:8*
Effects   *Luke 10:20; Heb. 12:23; Rev. 20:12–15*

Branch (Symbolic) (See also Growth, Vine)
Israel as   *Isa. 4:2; Rom. 11:17–24*
Christians and non-Christians as   *John 15:2–8*

Messiah as   *Isa. 11:1*

Bread (See also Communion, Food, Manna)
Unleavened, for Passover   *Exod. 12:15, 17–20*
In the tabernacle   *Lev. 24:5–9; Heb. 9:2*
Miraculous provision of   *1 Kings 17:6; Matt. 14:19–21*
Figurative, of Christ   *John 6:32–35, 48–51*
To commemorate Christ's sacrifice   *Luke 22:7, 19;*
    1 Cor. 22:23–29
Sharing of symbolizes fellowship   *Acts 2:42*

Breastplate (See also Armor)
For high priest   *Exod. 28:15–30*
Worn by soldiers   *1 Sam. 17:5*
Symbol of righteousness   *Isa. 59:17; Eph. 6:14*

Bribery
As sin   *Exod. 23:8; Ps. 26:10; Isa. 1:23; Amos 5:12*
Will be punished   *Amos 2:6*
■ Examples:
    Balak   *Num. 22:17, 37*
    Delilah   *Judg. 16:5*
    Soldiers   *Matt. 28:11–15*
    Unsuccessful by Simon Magus   *Acts 8:18*
    Hoped for by Felix   *Acts 24:25–26*

Bride (See also Bridegroom, Marriage, Wife)
Brings joy to husband   *Isa. 62:5*
Symbolizes Israel   *Ezek. 16:8–14*
Symbolizes church   *2 Cor. 11:2; Eph. 5:31–32*

Bridegroom (See also Bride, Husband, Marriage)
Rejoices over bride   *Isa. 62:5*
To separate from former home   *Gen. 2:24; Eph. 5:31*
Exempted from military duty   *Deut. 24:5*
Symbolizes God   *Isa. 62:5; Ezek. 16:8–14*
Symbolizes Christ   *2 Cor. 11:2; Eph. 5:31–32;*
    Rev. 21:2, 9

Brother (See also Family)
First example *Gen. 4:1–2*
A fellow Christian *Matt. 23:8; 1 Cor. 8:11; James 2:15*

Burial (See also Death)
Treatment of body *Gen. 50:26; Matt. 26:12; John 11:44*
Rites surrounding *Gen. 23:4–6; Jer. 34:5, John 11:19*
■ Famous:
  Abraham and Sarah *Gen. 23:19; 25:8–10*
  David *1 Kings 2:10*
  Jesus *John 19:38–42*

Burnt Offering (See also Offering, Sacrifice)
Atonement its purpose *Lev. 1:4*
Laws concerning *Lev. 1:11–17; 6:9–13; 17:8–9*
Offered during special feasts *Lev. 23:26–38*
Offered daily *Exod. 29:38–42; Num. 28:1–8*

Business (See also Commerce, Finances, Vocation)
■ Proper attitudes:
  Desire to put God first *Matt. 6:33; Col. 3:17, 23–24*
  Warnings about *Matt. 6:19–21; Luke 12:13–21, 34*
  Using gifts to the fullest *Rom. 12:8, 11*
  Freedom from anxiety *Matt. 6:25–34*
  Responsibility to tithe *Mal. 3:8–10*
■ Good examples:
  Joseph *Gen. 41:33–49*
  Officers and workmen *2 Chron. 34:8–13*
  Daniel *Dan. 6:1–5*
  Mordecai *Esther 10:2–3*

C

Caesarea

Home of Philip and Cornelius   *Acts 8:40; 10:1*
Home of Herod and Felix   *Acts 18:19–23; 23:23–24*
Peter preached there   *Acts 10:34–43*
Paul preached there   *Acts 9:30*
Paul imprisoned and tried there   *Acts 23:23–26:32*

Cain (See also Abel)

Life, sin, and punishment   *Gen. 4:1–17*
Called "of the evil one"   *1 John 3:12*

Calamity (See also Affliction, Suffering)

■ Kinds of:
  Personal, to Job   *Job 1:13–2:13*
  National, to Judah   *Lam. 1:1–22*
  World-wide   *Matt. 24:5–31; Luke 21:25–28*
■ Because of:
  Hardness of heart   *Exod. 7:20—12:30*
  Rebellion   *Num. 16:1–44*
  God's own purposes   *Job 1:1–2:6; 42:10–17*

Caleb

God-fearing spy   *Num. 13:1–2, 6, 26–30*
Honored by God   *Num. 14:24, 30, 36–38*
Received land in Canaan   *Josh. 14:6–15*

Calf

Offered in sacrifice   *Lev. 9:2–3; Mic. 6:6*
Aaron's golden idol   *Exod. 32:1–6*

Calling (See also Career, Election)

Obedience to one's   *1 Cor. 7:17–24*
From God   *Rom. 8:30; 11:29*
High, holy, heavenly   *Phil. 3:14; 2 Tim. 1:9; Heb. 3:1*
Goals of it   *Rom. 8:30; 1 Cor. 7:15; Gal. 5:13*

Calvary (See also Crucifixion, Jesus Christ)
Place where Christ was crucified   *Matt. 27:33*

Cana
Where Christ turned water into wine   *John 2:1-11*

Canaan
The land and God's promise   *Gen. 10:19, Exod. 3:8*
Its peoples   *Exod. 3:17*
God's promises concerning   *Gen. 15:16-21; 26:2-4*

Canaanites
Cursed descendants of Ham   *Gen. 9:25-26*
Idolatrous and wicked   *Lev. 18:24-27; Deut. 29:17-18*
Destroyed in judgment   *Exod. 23:23-33; Judg. 1:1-36*
Communion with Israel forbidden   *Deut. 7:2-3*

Capernaum
■ Christ's healing there:
   A centurion's servant   *Matt. 8:5-13*
   Peter's mother-in-law and others   *Mark 1:21-34*
   A paralytic   *Mark 2:1-12*
   A nobleman's son   *John 4:46-54*

Captivity (See also Bondage, Liberty, Servant)
■ Of Israel:
   In Egypt, foretold   *Gen. 15:13-14*
   In Egypt, fulfilled   *Exod. 1:1-14*
   In Assyria and Babylon, foretold   *Amos 7:11;*
      Isa. 39:6
   In Assyria and Babylon, fulfilled   *2 Kings 17:3-24;*
      24:10-25:21
   Because of idolatry and disobedience   *Deut.*
      28:36-38; Amos 5:25-27
■ Symbolic of being:
   Under Satan   *2 Tim. 2:26*
   In need of Christ   *Luke 4:18*

Care (See also Anxiety, Stress, Worry)
Of believers for one another   1 Cor. 12:25
Casting on Christ   1 Pet. 5:7
Christ's rebuke of Martha's   Luke 10:41
Of man in need   Luke 10:34
Reproof of anxiety   Phil. 4:6

Career (See also Business, Vocation)
Commit to the Lord   Prov. 16:3
Serve the Lord in   Col. 3:23-25
■ Showing good will:
  In service as to God   Eph. 6:7
  As employee   Eph. 6:8
  As employer   Eph. 6:9

Carmel, Mount
Hiding from God on   Amos 9:3
By the sea   Jer. 46:18
Showdown at   1 Kings 18:19
David weds Abigail of   1 Sam. 25:40
Elijah at   2 Kings 4:25

Celebration (See Dancing, Feast)

Celibacy (See also Asceticism, Marriage)
Paul wishes it for all men   1 Cor. 7:7
Benefit of remaining in   1 Cor. 7:8
Not a command from the Lord   1 Cor. 7:25
Though married   1 Cor. 7:29
Conducive to service   1 Cor. 7:32

Change (See also Corruption, Instability, Steadfastness)
God does not   Mal. 3:6
Of believers at resurrection   1 Cor. 15:51-52
Of believers into the Lord's likeness   2 Cor. 3:18
Of believers' bodies to glorious bodies   Phil. 3:21

Character (See also Growth, Integrity, Virtue)
List of good qualities   *2 Pet. 1:5-7*
Of a leader   *Titus 1:7-9*
Security of   *Prov. 10:9*
Which is controlled   *Prov. 16:32*
Boldness of   *Esther 4:16*
Fickleness of   *Luke 22:60-62*

Charity (See also Beneficence, Benevolence, Love)
Need to sustain the poor   *Lev. 25:35*
Blessings on those who practice   *Ps. 41:1*
Happiness for those who practice   *Prov. 14:21*
Required by Jesus   *Matt. 19:21*
Demonstrated by Paul   *Gal. 2:10*

Chastisement (See also Chiding, Discipline, Reproof)
Training by   *Heb. 12:11*
For those God loves   *Heb. 12:6*
Not to be despised   *Prov. 3:11*

Chastity (See also Celibacy, Purity)
Of wives   *1 Pet. 3:2*
Is will of God   *1 Thess. 4:3, 7*

Cherubim (See also Angels, Seraphim)
In the tabernacle   *Exod. 25:20*
In the temple   *1 Kings 6:23-28*
In Ezekiel's vision   *Ezek. 41:17-20, 25*

Chiding (See also Chastisement, Discipline)
Of Israelites by Moses   *Exod. 17:2*
Of the Lord   *Ps. 103:9*
By Martha   *Luke 10:40*

Chief Priest (See also Priest)
Office instituted   *Lev. 21:10-15*

Garments of   *Exod. 28:2–42*
Duties of   *Heb. 5:1–4*
Christ as   *Heb. 4:14–16*
Delivered Jesus to Pilate   *Matt. 27:1–2*

Children (See also Baby, Family)
■ Of God:
Power to become   *John 1:12*
Spirit bears witness that we are   *Rom. 8:16*
■ Symbolic:
Becoming as   *Matt. 18:2*
In understanding   *1 Cor. 14:20*
To obey parents   *Col. 3:20*

Choice (See also Acting Wisely, Decision,
Opportunity)
God made   *Acts 15:7; Eph. 1:4–5; 1 Thess. 1:4*
Of Stephen   *Acts 6:5*
Of Moses   *Ps. 106:23*

Christ (See also Jesus Christ)
Is the Son of God   *Matt. 16:16*
Needed to suffer   *Luke 26:26*
Demonstrated his love   *Rom. 5:8*
Is end of Law   *Rom. 10:4*
Is proclaimed   *Phil. 1:18*
Worth of knowing   *Phil. 3:8*
Righteousness through faith in   *Rom. 3:22*

Christian (See also Conversion, Disciple)
How to become   *John 3:16*
Characteristics of   *John 13:34–35; Gal. 5:22–24*
Suffering as   *1 Pet. 4:16*
First called   *Acts 11:26*

Christmas (See also Birth, Incarnation, Nativity)
Observance of Christ's birth   *Matt. 1:18–2:11*
Observance of God coming in flesh   *1 Tim. 3:16*

Church (See also Assembly, Body)
Building of   *Matt. 16:18; Eph. 2:20–21*
Head of   *Eph. 1:22*
Loved by Christ   *Eph. 5:25*
Persecuted by Paul   *Gal. 1:13*
The pillar and bulwark of truth   *1 Tim. 3:15*
Gifts of   *1 Cor. 12:27–30*

Circumcision
A sign of covenant   *Gen. 17:10*
Not required for Gentile converts   *Acts 15:1–21*
Faith replaces   *Gal. 5:6*
A matter of the heart   *Rom. 2:28–29*

Citizenship (See also Authority, Society)
Obligations of   *Rom. 13:1–7; 1 Pet. 2:13–17*
Punishment for neglect of   *Ezra 7:26*
Jesus discussed   *Matt. 17:24–27; 22:17–21*

Cleansing (See also Atonement, Sanitation, Washing)
■ Figurative of:
  Forgiveness of sin   *Ps. 51:7, 10; 1 John 1:7*

Cleopas
A disciple   *Luke 24:18*

Clothing
Figurative of unrighteousness   *Isa. 64:6*
Of women   *1 Tim. 2:9–10; 1 Pet. 3:3–4*
Ceremonial cleansing of   *Lev. 11:32*

Cloud
Rainbow in   *Gen. 9:13–16*
Pillar of   *Exod. 13:21–22*
Likening love to   *Hos. 6:4*
Christ returning in   *Luke 21:27*

Colosse
Paul's letter to the church at   *Col. 1:1–4:18*

Comfort (See also Comforter, Consolation)
Given to Job   *Job 2:11*
For God's people   *Isa. 40:1*
In bereavement   *John 11:19*
In Christ   *Phil. 2:1*

Comforter (See also Comfort, Holy Spirit)
Jesus promised   *John 14:16*
Is the Holy Spirit   *John 14:17*
Is teacher of all things   *John 14:26*
Convicts of sin   *John 16:8*
Is a guide   *John 16:13*
Brings glory to Christ   *John 16:14*

Commandments (See also Law, Ten Commandments)
Of God   *John 15:12*
■ Of Jesus:
  Examples of   *Matt. 5:16, 27–28, 31–32, 34*
Of a father   *Prov. 6:20; 7:1*

Commerce (See also Business, Finances, Work)
Misuse of   *Matt. 21:12–13*
Use of money from   *Luke 19:8*
Converts engaged in   *Acts 16:14; 18:2–3*
Cheating in   *Hos. 12:7*

Communion (See also Eucharist, Loaf, Lord's Supper)
Instituted by Christ   *1 Cor. 11:23–26*
Signified by bread and wine   *1 Cor. 10:16–17*
Christ's death proclaimed by   *1 Cor. 11:26*
Examining of heart before   *1 Cor. 11:27–29*
Early church observed   *Acts 2:42*

Communion of Saints (See also Fellowship, Unity)
In early church   Acts 2:42
Thanks for   Phil. 1:5
In Christ's love   Phil. 2:1-2
With God and Jesus Christ   John 17:21; 1 John 1:3
When walking in light   1 John 1:6-7

Compassion (See also Beneficence, Kindness, Pity)
Of God   Deut. 13:17; Ps. 78:38
Of Jesus   Matt. 9:36
Of Good Samaritan   Luke 10:33-34
As a mark of believers   1 Pet. 3:8

Complaining (See also Frustration, Impatience)
No need for   Ps. 144:14-15
Against God   Job 7:13-14
Bitterness of   Job. 23:2
Poured out to God   Ps. 102:1-11
Of the Jews against Paul   Acts 25:7

Compromise (See also Diplomacy)
Encouraged for one's own good   Prov. 25:8-10
In reconciliation   Matt. 5:24-25

Conceit (See also Arrogance, Boasting, Pride)
Attributed to fools   Prov. 26:5
One who has is hopeless   Prov. 26:12
Attributed to the lazy   Prov. 26:16
Not to characterize Christians   Rom. 12:16
Dangers of   1 Tim. 3:6

Condemnation (See also Punishment, Wrath)
Of man   John 3:19
Remedy for   John 5:24
Resulted from Adam's sin   Rom. 5:16

None for those in Christ   *Rom. 8:1*
Of Sodom and Gomorrah   *2 Pet. 2:6*

Conduct (See also Behavior, Guidance)
Of an elder   *1 Tim. 3:2-7*
Of a deacon   *1 Tim. 3:8-10*
Of wives   *Prov. 31:10-31; 1 Tim. 3:11; Titus 2:3-5*
Of older men   *Titus 2:2*
Of younger men   *Titus 2:6-7*

Confession
That Jesus is Lord   *Rom. 10:9-10; Phil. 2:11*
That Jesus is the Son of God   *1 John 4:15*
Of sins to God   *1 John 1:9*
To one another   *James 5:16*
Of evil practices   *Acts 19:18*
Of Christ before others   *Matt. 10:32-33*

Confidence (See also Boldness, Courage, Trust)
In the Son of God   *1 John 5:14-15*
In God   *1 Pet. 1:21*
Misplaced   *Mic. 7:5*
In self   *Phil. 3:4-8*

Confusion
None with God   *1 Cor. 14:33*
Of language at Babel   *Gen. 11:6-9*
God drove enemies into   *Exod. 23:27*
Jerusalem in   *Acts 21:31*

Conscience
Affirmation of a good   *Acts 23:1*
Maintaining a clear   *Acts 24:16*
Bears witness to God   *Rom. 2:15*
Of the weaker brother   *2 Cor. 8:12*
Maintains truth   *1 Tim. 3:9*
Cleansed by Christ   *Heb. 9:14*

Consecration (See also Dedication, Holiness, Sanctification)

Of priests *Exod. 29:1–46*
Of Christ *Heb. 10:20*
Of believers *Rom. 12:1–2; 2 Cor. 8:5*

Consideration (See also Kindness)

To the poor *Ps. 41:1; Prov. 29:7*
Of sin *Ezek. 18:28*

Consolation (See also Comfort, Compassion)

Attribute of God *Rom. 15:5*
In Christ *Phil. 2:1*
Of Paul *Philem. 7*
Of Israel *Luke 2:25*

Contentment (See also Anxiety, Peace)

With what one has *Heb. 13:5*
In any situation *Phil. 4:11*
Of mind *Isa. 26:3*
In believing in Christ *Rom. 15:13*
Through walking by the Spirit *Gal. 5:22*

Conversation (See also Mouth, Speech, Tongue)

Should be honest *1 Pet. 2:12*
Should be edifying *Eph. 4:29–5:4*
Should be gracious *Col. 4:6*

Conversion (See also Regeneration, Repentance)

■ Of sinners:
  Turned from idols *1 Thess. 1:9*
  Become new creatures *2 Cor. 5:17*
Comes from God through Christ *2 Cor. 5:18–19*
Repentance needed for *Acts 2:38*
Of Paul *Acts 9:22, 26*
Of Gentiles *Acts 15:3*

Conviction of Sin (See also Guilt, Remorse, Sin)

The Law brings   *Rom. 2:15*
The Holy Spirit brings   *John 16:7–8*
Through Peter's sermon   *Acts 2:37*
Comes from God   *Job 33:27–30*

Corinth

■ Paul's contact with:
   Travelled to   *Acts 18:1*
   Wrote the church there   *1 Cor. 1:2*
   Did not visit again   *2 Cor. 1:23–2:4*
Apollos visited   *Acts 11:1*

Cornelius

His vision and call for Peter   *Acts 10:1–8*
Peter's sermon at his house   *Acts 10:34–48*

Cornerstone (See also Foundation)

Figuratively, Christ is the   *Matt. 21:42; Eph. 2:20*

Corruption (See also Disease, Health, Sickness)

Christ's flesh did not see   *Acts 2:31*
Creation will be freed from   *Rom. 8:21*
Of the world   *2 Pet. 1:4*

Counsel

Of the wicked   *Ps. 1:1; Prov. 12:5*
Of the Lord   *Ps. 16:7; Isa. 28:29*
Accepted by the wise   *Prov. 12:15; 19:20*
Rejecting God's   *Prov. 1:28–30*
A Christian's role to give   *Rom. 15:14*

Courage (See also Boldness, Confidence)

Call to   *Deut. 31:7; Josh. 1:6–9; Ps. 27:14*
From seeing friends   *Acts 28:15*
Paul testified to having   *2 Cor. 5:6–8*

Courts
Instructions regarding   *Exod. 23:1-8*
Justice required of   *Deut. 1:16-17*
Abiding by sentence of   *Deut. 17:8-12*

Covenant (See also Promise, Vow)
Between God and Noah   *Gen. 9:12-15*
Between God and Abraham   *Gen. 17:1-8*
Between God and the Israelites   *Exod. 19:3-6*
Christ brought a new one   *Heb. 8:6-13; 10:18; 12:24*

Covetousness (See also Avarice, Envy, Greed)
Against God's decree   *Exod. 20:17*
Jesus' instruction against   *Luke 12:15*
Against Paul's teaching   *Col. 3:5*

Cowardice (See also Courage, Fear)
■ Shown by:
Israel's spies   *Num. 13:30-31*
Jonah   *Jon. 1:1-3*
Pilate   *John 19:12-16*
Peter   *John 18:15-18*

Creation (See also Earth, World)
Account of   *Gen. 1:1-2:25*
Work of the Lord   *Ps. 104:1-35*
Work of the Word   *John 1:1-14*
Work of the Son   *Col. 1:13-17; Heb. 1:1-3*

Creativity (See also Art)
Used for God's purposes   *Gen. 35:4-38:23*

Crime (See also Law, Sin, Ten Commandments)
Murder of Abel   *Gen. 4:8-9*
Selling of Joseph   *Gen. 37:26-28*
Murder of Abner   *2 Sam. 3:22-29*
Deceit of Ananias and Sapphira   *Acts 5:1-6*

Cheating of Zaccheus   *Luke 19:1–8*

Cross (See also Atonement, Crucifixion, Redemption)

Bearing of   *John 19:17*
Death on   *Mark 15:22–26; John 19:16–37*
Prediction of   *John 3:14–15*

Crown (See also King)

■ Literal:
 Worn by the high priest   *Lev. 8:9*
 Worn by the kings   *2 Sam. 12:30*
■ Figurative:
 Of a virtuous woman   *Prov. 12:4*
 Of children   *Prov. 17:6*
■ Rewards:
 ˙For the Apostle Paul   *Phil. 4:1*
 For adherence to principles   *2 Tim. 2:5*

Crucifixion (See also Atonement, Redemption, Resurrection)

■ Literal:
 Prediction   *Matt. 20:19; John 12:32*
 Time of   *John 19:14*
 Event   *Mark 15:22–26; John 19:16–37*
■ Figurative:
 Union with Christ   *Rom. 6:5; Gal. 2:20*

Cruelty (See also Beating)

Characteristic of the wicked   *Ps. 37:14*
To animals   *Num. 22:27–35*
■ Example of:
 Herod the Great   *Matt. 2:13–16*
 To the faithful   *Heb. 11:35–38*
 The Judaizers   *Acts 14:19*

Curiosity
Eve and the tree of life   *Gen. 3:6*
Zaccheus'   *Luke 19:1-6*
Jews' questioning of John the Baptist   *John 1:19-27*
Athenians'   *Acts 17:21*

Curse (See also Damnation, Oath)
On Cain's farming   *Gen. 4:11-13*
On Israel's disobedience   *Deut. 28:15-45*
On Jericho's rebuilders   *Josh. 6:26*
Jesus' on the fig tree   *Mark 11:12-14, 20-21*

Cyrus
King of Persia   *2 Chron. 36:22*
Prophecies concerning   *Isa. 44:28; 45:1*

D
Damaris
Young woman who followed Paul   *Acts 17:34*

Damascus
Abraham's journey   *Gen. 14:15*
David's victory   *2 Sam. 8:5-6*
■ In Paul's life:
Journey to   *Acts 9:1-9*
Conversion at   *Acts 9:10-19*
Escapes from   *2 Cor. 11:32-33*

Damnation (See also Curse, Punishment)
For blasphemy against the Holy Spirit   *Mark 3:29*
Against Scribes and Pharisees   *Matt. 23:14*
■ Of:
Faithless   *Rom. 14:23*
Evil doers   *Rom. 3:8*
Resurrected   *John 5:29*

Dan
Son of Jacob   *Gen. 30:6*
Blessed by Jacob   *Gen. 49:16*
Tribe idolatrous   *Judg. 18:30; 1 Kings 12:29*

Dancing
By worshipers   *Ps. 149:3*
By children   *Matt. 11:16-17*
Because of victory over enemies   *1 Sam. 18:6-7*
Because of son's return   *Luke 15:22-25*
By daughter of Herodias   *Matt. 14:6*

Danger
■ Examples of:
Jesus and the disciples at sea   *Luke 8:22-25*

Paul's perilous voyage   *Acts 27:9–44*
Paul's afflictions   *2 Cor. 11:23–33*
Paul's escape from   *Acts 9:22–25*
Spiritual neglect is   *Heb. 2:1–3*

Daniel (See also Prophecy, Prophet)
Taken to Babylon   *Dan. 1:1–7*
Interpreted dreams   *Dan. 2:1–45*
Interpreted handwriting   *Dan. 5:10–29*
Honored by rulers   *Dan. 2:46–49; 6:1–3, 23–28*
Cast into the lion's den   *Dan. 6:6–22*
Saw visions   *Dan. 7:1–14*

Darius
Became king of Babylon   *Dan. 5:30–31*
Had Daniel put in lion's den   *Dan. 6:16*
Decreed worship of Daniel's God   *Dan. 6:25–27*

Darkness (See also Blindness, Light)
Before the world existed   *Gen. 1:2–4*
The plague of   *Exod. 10:21–22*
The righteous as light in   *Ps. 112:4*
At the death of Christ   *Matt. 27:45*
Fruitless deeds of   *Eph. 5:11*

Daughter (See also Family, Son)
The ideal   *Prov. 31:29*
A loyal   *Ruth 1:12–18*
A beautiful   *Ps. 45:9–13*

David
Genealogy of   *1 Chron. 2:3–15*
Shepherd   *1 Sam. 16:11–12*
Slayer of Goliath   *1 Sam. 17:4, 49*
Chosen of God   *1 Sam. 16:1, 13*
King over Judah, Israel   *2 Sam. 2:1–4, 11; 5:1–5*
Faith of   *Heb. 11:32–33*

Day (See also Night)
Creation of   *Gen. 1:5, 16*
Of the Lord   *Jer. 45:10; 1 Thess. 5:2*
Symbol of the present age   *Heb. 1:2*

Deacon (See also Elder, Servant)
Ordination by the apostles   *Acts 6:1–6*
Listed with the elders   *Phil. 1:1*
Qualifications of   *1 Tim. 3:8–13*
Phoebe a female   *Rom. 16:1*

Dead Sea
Salt sea   *Num. 34:3, 12*
Sea of the Plain   *Deut. 3:17*
South boundary of Judah   *Josh. 15:2, 5*

Deafness
Protection of the Lord   *Lev. 19:14*
Healing by the Lord   *Matt. 11:5; Mark 7:37*
■ Spiritual:
Of man   *Ps. 38:13*
Of Israel   *Isa. 42:18*

Death (See also Bereavement, Burial, Mortality)
■ Eternal:
Result of God's wrath   *1 Thess. 1:10*
Second death   *Rev. 20:14*
■ Natural:
Consequence of sin   *Gen. 3:3; Rom. 5:12*
Termination of earthly life   *Eccles. 9:10*
Return to dust   *Gen. 3:19*
Lot of all men   *Heb. 9:27*

Deborah
Prophetess who judged and delivered Israel   *Judg. 4:4–24*
Her song   *Judg. 5:1–31*

Debt, Debtor (See also Money)

Usury prohibited   *Deut. 23:19–20; Ezek. 18:8–17*
Parable of Jesus   *Matt. 18:23–35*
■ Figuratively:
   Of sin   *Matt. 6:12*
   Moral obligation   *Rom. 1:14*

Deceit (See also Lying)

■ Examples:
   Isaac   *Gen. 26:7*
   David   *1 Sam. 21:12–13*
   Ananias   *Acts 5:1–11*
The wicked's pleasure   *Prov. 20:17*
Of servants of Satan   *2 Cor. 11:14*
The sign of the antichrist   *1 John 4:1–6*

Decision (See also Choice, Guidance)

To believe God   *Heb. 11:6*
To serve the Lord   *Josh. 24:15*
To continue in the faith   *1 Cor. 16:13, Acts 14:22*
To resist the devil   *James 4:7*
To not follow Christ   *Luke 18:18–23*

Decrees (See also Law)

For teaching   *Exod. 18:20*
That are just and unjust   *Prov. 8:15; Isa. 10:1–2*
Resisting   *Rom. 13:2*
Submission to   *1 Pet. 2:13*

Dedication (See also Consecration, Holiness)

Of the altar   *Num. 7:1–3*
For service   *Judg. 5:2*
Of God's house   *2 Chron. 2:4*
Of lives   *Rom. 12:1*

Defilement (See also Apostasy, Sin)

Ceremonial   *Mark 7:1–4*

Comes from the heart   *Mark 7:14–23*
Of deceivers and rebels   *Jude 8*

Delilah
Lover of Samson who betrayed him   *Judg. 16:4–21*

Deliverance, Divine (See also Bondage, Salvation)
God provides   *Ps. 32:7; 116:6*
Of apostles from prison   *Acts 5:18–19*
Of Paul from torture   *2 Tim. 4:17*
From evil   *Matt. 6:13*
Through prayers and the Spirit   *Phil. 1:19*

Demetrius
Silversmith   *Acts 19:24*
Disciple   *3 John 12*

Demon (See also Devil, Evil, Exorcism)
Worship of denounced   *Deut. 32:16–17; 1 Tim. 4:1*
Possession by   *Matt. 8:28–34; Mark 7:25–30*
Cast out by Jesus   *Matt. 4:24; 8:16*
Cast out by Peter   *Acts 5:16*
Cast out by Paul   *Acts 19:12*
To be punished   *2 Pet. 2:4*

Dependency
On God   *Ps. 37:5; 20:7–8; Prov. 3:5–6*
Of Paul on the Lord   *1 Cor. 4:3–4*
On riches   *Mark 10:23*

Depression (See also Anxiety, Despair)
■ Examples of:
  David   *Ps. 22:1–2*
  Ezra   *Ezra 10:1, 6*
  Peter   *Matt. 26:75*
Counsel concerning   *Ps. 34:18; 42:11; Zeph 3:17; Rom. 8:31; 12:12*

Desertion (See also Abandonment)

Saved from   *Ps. 16:10*
From the truth by believers   *Gal. 1:6*
Of many disciples   *John 6:67*

Desire (See also Motive)

Of God for man   *Hos. 6:6*
For heaven   *Heb. 11:14*
For spiritual gifts   *1 Cor. 14:1*
To accomplish   *Prov. 13:19*
Of the righteous   *Prov. 10:24*
Of the flesh   *Gal. 5:17; Eph. 2:3*

Despair

Personal   *Num. 11:15; Job 10:1*
From doing wrong   *Luke 22:61–62*
Of Jesus   *Mark 15:34*

Devil (See also Evil, Lucifer, Satan, Serpent)

Deceived Eve   *Gen. 3:1–5*
Temptation of Jesus by   *Matt. 4:1–10*
Christians to resist   *James 4:7*
■ Names of:
  Deceiver, ancient serpent, great dragon   *Rev. 12:9*
  Angel of light   *2 Cor. 11:14*
  Beelzebub   *Matt. 10:25*

Devotion (See also Dedication, Sanctification)

To God's will   *Matt. 7:21*
Of Christ   *Luke 22:42; 2 Cor. 8:9*
To characterize Christians   *Col. 1:2*
Between friends   *1 Sam. 18:1–3*

Diet (See also Food)

Of Daniel   *Dan. 1:8–16*
No blood in Israelites'   *Lev. 17:12*
Of Nazirite   *Num. 6:3–4*

Diligence (See also Work)

In obeying   *Zech. 6:15*
To be added to faith   *2 Pet. 1:5–7*
In behavior   *1 Pet. 2:12*

Diplomacy (See also Ambassador, Compromise)

Of Abigail   *1 Sam. 25:28–34*
Of Abraham and Abimelech   *Gen. 21:22–23*
Of Paul   *Acts 16:3; 1 Cor. 9:20–23*

Disciple (See also Apostle, Christian, Discipleship)

Of Jesus   *Matt. 10:1–4; Luke 10:1–11*
First called Christians in Antioch   *Acts 11:26*
Known by love for others   *John 13:35*
Bears fruit as proof   *John 15:8*

Discipleship (See also Devotion, Disciple, Growth)

Responsibility of   *2 Tim. 2:2–8*
Characterized by love   *John 21:15–18*
The cost of   *Luke 14:25–33*

Discipline (See also Chastisement, Chiding, Reproof)

By parents   *Prov. 19:18; 23:13*
By God   *Heb. 12:5–11*
■ In the church:
  Of those who sin   *1 Tim. 5:20*
  Of restoring one to fellowship   *Gal. 6:1*
  Of warning the unruly   *1 Tim. 6:4–5*
  Of false teachers   *1 Tim. 6:3*

Discretion (See also Prudence, Tact)

Of Joseph   *Gen. 41:39–40*
In youth   *Prov. 5:2*
Desired by David for Solomon   *1 Chron. 22:12*

Disease (See also Corruption, Health)
As judgment   Num. 12:9-10; 2 Chron. 21:18
Inflicted by Satan   Job 2:7
Prayer for healing of   2 Kings 20:3-11
Healed by Christ   Matt. 4:23; John 5:8-9
Healed by disciples   Luke 9:1; Acts 3:2-7

Dishonesty (See also Lying, Treachery)
Against the poor   Job 24:3-4; Ezek. 22:29
In business   Amos 8:5
Punishment for   Zeph. 1:9; Zech. 5:3-4

Disobedience (See also Obedience, Rebellion)
To God   Exod. 5:2; 1 Kings 13:21
To covenant   Jer. 11:3
To the truth   Gal. 3:1
Children of   Eph. 5:6
To the gospel   2 Thess. 1:8
In neglect of salvation   Heb. 2:3

Divorce (See also Marriage)
Jesus' teaching on   Matt. 5:32; 19:9; Mark 10:10-12
Because of hardness of heart   Mark 10:5-9
Paul's view of   1 Cor. 7:27

Doctrine (See also Law, Teaching)
■ Of Jesus:
  Came from the Father   John 7:16-17
  Questioned by high priest   John 18:19
For Christian training   2 Tim. 3:16
Paul's defense of   Acts 24:14-15
Warning against false   Rom. 16:17-18

Dorcas
Raised from dead by Peter   Acts 9:40

Doubt
In trials *Mark 4:40; 1 Pet. 1:6*
Mixed with faith *James 1:6–8*
In belief *John 20:25–29*
Leads to unbelieving heart *Heb. 3:12*

Dream (See also Vision)
- Used by God:
  To teach *Gen. 28:13–15; Matt. 1:20–21*
  To warn *Gen. 41:14–32*
  To guide *Matt. 2:13*

Dress (See Apparel, Clothing)

Drinking (See also Drunkenness, Wine)
- Abstaining from wine:
  Priests *Lev. 10:8–10*
  Nazirites *Num. 6:3*
Results of *Prov. 23:21, 29–30, 33–35*
Temperance in *Eph. 5:18*
At wedding *John 2:3, 9–10*
As an offense to others *Rom. 14:21*

Drunkenness (See also Abstinence from Alcohol, Wine)
Leads to poverty *Prov. 23:21*
Burdened by *Luke 21:34*
None in kingdom of God *1 Cor. 6:10*
Is debauchery *Eph. 5:18*

Duty (See also Obligation, Responsibility, Servant)
To worship God *1 Chron. 16:28–30*
To do right in God's sight *Deut. 6:18*
To do good to others *Prov. 3:27*
Of Jesus to God *Luke 2:49*
To government *Rom. 13:6–7*
To love *Rom. 13:8*

E

Ear

Made by God for listening   *Prov. 20:12*
The wise use it for knowledge   *Prov. 18:15*
Blessed are those who use it   *Rev. 1:3*

Earth (See also Creation, World)

Created by God   *Gen. 1:1*
To be inhabited   *Isa. 45:13*
God brought judgments on   *Gen. 3:14–19*
Supreme authority of   *Matt. 28:18*
■ Vision of a new:
   God and his people will be there   *Rev. 21:3*
   No death and no tears   *Rev. 21:4*

Easter

Sunday commemorating Resurrection   *John 20:1–18*

Eden

Garden of   *Gen. 2:8*
Adam driven from   *Gen. 3:24*

Edom

Land of Esau   *Gen. 32:3*
Prophecies concerning   *Isa. 34:5; Jer. 25:21; Ezek.
   25:13; Amos 1:11*

Egypt (See also Pharaoh)

Joseph made a ruler of   *Gen. 41:44*
Israel in bondage to   *Exod. 1:8–14*
Plagues brought on   *Exod. 7:17–11:10*
God delivered Israelites from   *Exod. 14:30*

Elder (See also Bishop, Deacon)

■ Of the church:
   Qualifications of   *Titus 1:6–9*

Appointed by local church   *Acts 14:23*
Participates in local church decisions   *Acts 15:6-29*
Willingly leads believers   *1 Peter 5:2-3*
Ministers to the sick   *James 5:14-15*

Eleazar
Son of Aaron and chief priest   *Exod. 6:23*
Son of Abinadab   *1 Sam. 7:1*
One of David's captains   *2 Sam. 23:9*

Election (See also Call, Predestination)
■ Of believers:
According to God's call and purpose   *Rom. 9:11*
Before the world began   *Eph. 1:4*
By grace   *Rom. 11:5*
For God's glory   *Eph. 1:6*
Through faith   *2 Thess. 2:13*

Eli
Trained the boy Samuel   *1 Sam. 1:25-28; 2:11*

Eliakim
Chief minister of Hezekiah   *2 Kings 18:18-37*

Elihu
Reproved Job's friends   *Job 32:2-37:24*

Elijah
Prophet persecuted by King Ahab   *1 Kings 17:2-3*
Fed by ravens   *1 Kings 17:4*
Brought to life widow's son   *1 Kings 17:17-24*
Contest with Baal worshipers   *1 Kings 18:19-40*
Predicted drought   *1 Kings 17:1*
Went to heaven in a whirlwind   *2 Kings 2:11*

Elisha
Successor to Elijah   *1 Kings 19:16*

E

Was given Elijah's cloak   *2 Kings 2:13*
- Miracles of:
  Brought child back to life   *2 Kings 4:32–35*
  Healed Naaman the leper   *2 Kings 5:9–14*

Elizabeth
Wife of Zechariah   *Luke 1:5*
Childless until old age   *Luke 1:7*
Mother of John the Baptist   *Luke 1:13*
Visited by Mary   *Luke 1:39*
Filled with the Holy Spirit   *Luke 1:41*

Emmaus
Christ talked to disciples on road to   *Luke 24:15*

Employee (See also Business, Duty, Work)
Not to be oppressed   *Deut. 24:14*
To be paid on time   *Deut. 24:15*
Deserves to be paid   *Luke 10:7; 1 Tim. 5:18*

Employer (See also Employee)
To pay for services   *Jer. 22:13*
Indebted to his workers   *Rom. 4:4*
To treat employees justly   *Col. 4:1*

Enemy
Do good to and love   *Luke 6:35*
Help when in trouble   *Exod. 23:4–5*
Pray for   *Matt. 5:44*
Last to be destroyed   *1 Cor. 15:26*
Of the cross   *Phil. 3:18–19*

Enoch
His dedication   *Gen. 5:18*
His faith   *Heb. 11:5*
Did not die   *Gen. 5:24*

Envy (See also Contentment, Covetousness, Jealousy)

Instructed to avoid   *1 Pet. 2:1*
Chief priests showed   *Mark 15:10*
Toward the wicked   *Prov. 24:19*
Toward the violent   *Prov. 3:31*
Leads to evil   *James 3:16*

Ephesus

■ Paul's contact with:
　Visited twice by Paul   *Acts 18:18-21; 19:1*
　Laid hands on disciples   *Acts 19:6*
　Spoke in synagogue   *Acts 19:8*
　Performed miracles   *Acts 19:11-12*
　Where believers gave up magic   *Acts 19:18-19*

Ephraim

Second son of Joseph   *Gen. 41:52*
Tribe of Israel   *Gen. 49:25*
Moses blessed   *Deut. 33:13-17*
Worshiped Baal   *Hos. 13:1*
Sin noted   *Hos. 13:12*

Esau

Twin son of Isaac and Rebecca   *Gen. 25:19-26*
Sold his birthright for food   *Gen. 25:29-34*
Cheated out of father's blessing   *Gen. 27:30-36*

Esther

Raised by Mordecai, her cousin   *Esther 2:7*
Chosen as queen   *Esther 2:17*
Interceded for her people, the Jews   *Esther 8:3-8*

Eternal Life (See Life, Salvation)

Eternity (See also Immortality, Heaven, Hell)

God inhabits   *Isa. 57:15*

God put into man's mind   *Eccles. 3:11*
The Lord will reign for   *Exod. 15:18*
Believers will live for   *Ps. 23:6*
Rewards in   *Matt. 19:28-30*
God's promise of life in   *1 John 2:25*

Ethics (See also Conduct, Morality)
Christians obliged to practice   *Prov. 14:2; Titus 2:12*
For employers   *Col. 4:1*
For employees   *Col. 3:23*
For citizens   *Rom. 13:1-7*
For God's glory   *Matt. 5:16*

Ethiopia
Prophecies concerning   *Ps. 68:31; Isa. 18:20*

Eucharist (See also Communion, Lord's Supper)
Instituted by Christ   *Matt. 26:26-28; Mark 14:22-24*
Observed by early church   *Acts 2:42, 46*
Preparing for   *1 Cor. 11:27-29*

Eunice
Mother of Timothy   *2 Tim. 1:5*

Eutychus
Young man raised from dead by Paul   *Acts 20:7-12*

Evangelism (See also Gospel, Witness, Mission)
Some believers have gift of   *Eph. 4:11*
Paul charged Timothy to do   *2 Tim. 4:5*
Of Paul to the Gentiles   *Eph. 3:8*
To be worldwide   *Mark 13:10*

Eve (See also Adam, Fall of Man)
Created by God   *Gen. 2:20-23*
Deceived by serpent   *Gen. 3:1-7*
Curse pronounced on   *Gen. 3:16*
Children of   *Gen. 4:1-2, 25; 5:3-4*

Evil (See also Abomination, Motive, Sin)
Source of   *Gen. 3:1–6*
God's attitude toward   *Rom. 1:18*
Doers of   *Ps. 37:1–2*
Examples of   *1 Sam. 19:1, 10; Rom. 1:29–31*
Returned for good   *1 Sam. 25:21*
Turning from   *Jer. 18:8*
Appearance of   *1 Thess. 5:22*

Exodus (See also Moses, Red Sea)
Israel's deliverance from Egypt   *Exod. 12:41–42*
Led by Moses   *Exod. 3:7–10; Acts 7:20–36*

Exorcism (See also Deliverance, Demon)
Practiced by Christ   *Matt. 8:16*
Power given disciples   *Matt. 10:1*
Attempted by others   *Acts 19:13*

Eye (See also Vision)
Of the Lord   *Ps. 33:18; Amos 9:8*
Lust of   *1 John 2:16*
Lamp of body   *Luke 11:34*

Ezekiel
Priest in Babylonian exile   *Ezek. 1:1–13*
Saw God's glory in a vision   *Ezek. 1:26–28*
Called son of man   *Ezek. 2:1*
Prophesied to rebellious Israel   *Ezek. 2:3–5*
Acted out the coming destruction   *Ezek. 4:1–8*

Ezra
Scribe and priest   *Ezra 7:11*
■ Commissioned by King of Persia:
    To lead group of Jews to Jerusalem   *Ezra 7:12–13*
    To carry treasures to temple   *Ezra 7:15–16*
Read the law to the people   *Ezra 8:2–3*
Spoke against marriage to heathen   *Ezra 10:10–11*

F

Face (See also Anthropomorphism)

Of God   *Ex. 33:23*
■ Representing God's look:
Of favor   *Num. 6:25*
Of disfavor   *Ps. 34:16*
Of Christ   *Matt. 17:2*

Failure (See also Despair, Shame)

Prayer to prevent   *Luke 22:32*

Faith (See also Belief, Witness)

Gift of God   *Eph. 2:8*
Condition of salvation   *Acts 16:31*
Way of life   *Eph. 6:16*
Author of   *Heb. 12:2*
Object of   *John 14:1*
Trial of   *James 1:3*

Faithfulness (See also Steadfastness, Long-suffering)

Seen in God   *Lam. 3:23; 1 Cor. 10:13*
Required in believers   *Rev. 2:10*
In service   *1 Cor. 4:2*
In all things   *Luke 16:10*

Fall of Man (See also Sin)

Through Satan's tempting   *Gen. 3:1-5*
Man's state as a result   *Rom. 3:23*
Remedy for, only in Christ   *Eph. 2:1-8*

Family (See also Brother, Father, Mother)

Established before the Fall   *Gen. 2:23-24*
■ Responsibilities of:
Wives   *Col. 3:18; Prov. 31:11-15*
Husbands   *Col. 3:19*

Children   *Col. 3:20*
Fathers   *Col. 3:21*
Mothers   *Prov. 31:15, 27–28*

Famine (See also Agriculture, Food)
Pharaoh warned of in dreams   *Gen. 41:1–40*
Experienced spiritually   *2 Chron. 15:3; Amos 8:11*
■ Caused by:
Enemies   *Deut. 28:49–51; 2 Kings 6:24–25*
Insects   *Joel 1:4*
Hail storms   *Exod. 9:23, 31*
Sin   *Ezek. 14:12–13*
■ Occurred in time of:
Abraham   *Gen. 12:10*
Isaac   *Gen. 26:1*
David   *2 Sam. 21:1*
Early Church   *Acts 11:28*

F

Farming (See also Agriculture)
Introduced by God   *Gen. 2:15*
Illustrations, parables based on   *Matt. 13:3–8*

Fasting (See also Asceticism, Food)
Jesus teaching on   *Matt. 6:16–18; Matt. 9:15*
For special needs   *Acts 14:23*
Accompanied by prayer   *Acts 13:3*
Not merely as a form   *Isa. 58:5–7*

Fatherhood (See also Motherhood)
Of God to all he created   *Deut. 32:6*
Of God to all who believe in his Son   *Gal. 4:4–6*
Of God to Jesus Christ   *Col. 1:3*

Fatigue (See also Sleep, Stress)
■ Examples of:
Christ and disciples   *Mark 6:30–31*
Christ en route to the cross   *Luke 23:26*
Help from the Lord in   *Isa. 40:31*

Fear (See also Anxiety, Worry)

Reverential, in worship to God   *Heb. 12:28*
Commanded of all   *Ps. 33:8*
As beginning of wisdom   *Job 28:28*
Dread of future   *Prov. 10:24; Luke 21:26*

Feast

At a wedding   *John 2:1–10*
Given by kings   *Esther 1:3*
At a coronation   *1 Chron. 12:38–39*
On occasion of national deliverance   *Esther 8:17*
Parable of   *Luke 14:7–13*

Felix

Governor of Judea   *Acts 23:23*
Paul's defense before   *Acts 24:10*
Convicted by preaching, but didn't release Paul   *Acts 24:24–27*

Fellowship (See also Communion of Saints, Unity)

- With God:
  For those who love him   *John 14:23*
  For those who obey him   *1 John 3:24*
- With Christ:
  For those gathered in his name   *Matt. 18:20*
- Of the Holy Spirit:
  For those who belong to Christ   *Rom. 8:9*

Festival (See Feast)

Festus

Governor of Judea after Felix   *Acts 24:27*
Paul's trial before   *Acts 25:6–12*

Fighting (See also Quarrel, Strife)

Contending for the faith   *1 Tim. 6:12*
Against afflictions   *2 Cor. 7:5*

Finances (See also Commerce, Money)
Cheating in *Amos 8:4–6*
Preparation in *1 Cor. 16:1–2*
Sharing in *2 Cor. 9:7*

Fire (See also Judgment)
■ Represents:
Cleansing *Isa. 6:6–7*
Spiritual power *Matt. 3:11*
Judgment *Rev. 20:9*
Everlasting punishment *Mark 9:48*

Firstborn (See also Birthright, Inheritance)
Consecrated to God *Exod. 13:2*
Death of *Exod. 11:5*
Christ described as *Col. 1:15*

Firstfruits (See also Offering)
■ Of harvest:
Required as offering *Exod. 22:29*
As wave offering *Lev. 23:20*
As thank offering on entering Promised Land
Deut. 26:1–4

Fish
Created *Gen. 1:20–22*
Jonah swallowed by *Jon. 1:17*
Big catch of *Luke 5:4–9*
Used in miracles *Matt. 14:19*

Flattery (See also Honesty, Mouth)
Description of those who engage in it *Ps. 5:9*
Purpose condemned *Jude 16*
Used to pressure *Prov. 7:21*
Related to condition of heart *Ps. 12:2*
Results of *Prov. 26:28*

Flesh (See also Body, Sin, Spirit)
Physical man   Gen. 2:23-24
Represents sinful nature of man   Eph. 2:3
Works against the Spirit   Gal. 5:17
Desires of, results in   Gal. 5:19-21
Christ took form of   John 1:14

Food (See also Diet, Drinking, Feast)
Provided by God for man   Gen. 1:29-30
For strength and satisfaction   Ps. 104:15
To abstain from   Gen. 2:16-17
Disciples concerned about   Matt. 14:15-17
Christ provided through miracle   Matt. 14:19-20
Christ gave thanks for   Mark 8:6

Foolishness
Seen by God   Ps. 69:5
Of a child   Prov. 22:15
Results of   Prov. 19:3
As sin   Prov. 24:9
■ To unbelievers:
  Preaching of Cross is   1 Cor. 1:18
  Things of God are   1 Cor. 2:14

Foreigner
Those who don't understand   1 Cor. 14:11
One who thanked Jesus   Luke 17:18
Figuratively, believers no longer are   Eph. 3:19

Forgiveness (See also Reconciliation, Redemption, Repentance)
■ Of man's sin:
  By God   Ps. 130:4
  By Christ   Acts 10:43
Among believers   Eph. 4:32
Of enemies   Luke 6:27

Formalism (See also Pharisees)
Vain worship   *Isa. 29:13*
Denounced by Christ   *Matt. 15:7-9*
In the last days   *2 Tim. 3:5*

Fornication (See also Adultery, Immorality, Lust)
Forbidden by God   *Exod. 20:14*
Punishment for   *Lev. 20:10; Heb. 13:4*
Christians to abstain from   *1 Thess. 4:3*

Foundation (See also Steadfastness, Stone)
■ Of the world:
    Laid by God   *Job 38:4*
    It is firm   *2 Tim. 2:19*
    No other but Christ   *1 Cor. 3:11*
    Building on it   *1 Cor. 3:12-14*

Friendship (See also Affection, Fellowship, Hospitality)
■ With God:
    For those who fear him   *Ps. 25:14*
■ Warnings against:
    With the angry   *Prov. 22:24*
    With the world   *James 4:4*
Betrayal in   *Ps. 41:9*
Agreement necessary in   *Amos 3:3*
A continuing relationship   *Prov. 17:17*

Fruit of the Spirit (See also Growth)
Described   *Gal. 3:23-24*

Frustration (See also Impatience)
■ Examples of:
    Jesus' expression of   *Matt. 23:37*
    Paul's expression of   *Rom. 7:15-25*

G

Gabriel (See also Angels)

- Angel who appeared:
  To Daniel   *Dan. 9:21*
  To Zacharias   *Luke 1:11-20*
  To Mary   *Luke 1:26-28*

Gad

Jacob's son   *Gen. 30:11*
Tribe blessed by Moses   *Deut. 33:20*
Commended by Joshua   *Josh. 22:1*
Charged with idolatry   *Josh. 22:11*
Their defense   *Josh 22:21*

Galilee

District in Israel   *Matt. 2:22*
City of refuge in   *Josh 20:7*
Prophecy of   *Isa. 9:1*
Herod, king of   *Mark 6:21*
Disciples from   *Acts 1:11*
Jesus taught and healed in   *Matt. 4:23*

Gamaliel

Paul brought up at feet of   *Acts 22:3*
Advised the council   *Acts 5:34*

Gates (See also Wall)

Of cities   *Deut. 3:5*
- Place for:
  Meetings   *Neh. 8*
  Judging offenses   *Deut. 21:19-20*
  Business   *Gen. 23:10*
- Figurative:
  Of righteousness   *Ps. 118:19*
  Of heaven   *Gen. 28:17*
  Of death   *Job 38:17*

Gath
City of Philistia   *1 Sam. 17:4*
Home of Goliath   *1 Sam. 17:4*

Gaza
Samson carried away gates of   *Judg. 16:1-3*
Destruction foretold   *Jer. 47:1-7; Amos 1:6*

Genealogy (See also Ancestor)
Of Jesus Christ   *Matt. 1:1-16*
Of the Jews   *Ezra 7:1-5; 8:1-15; Neh. 7; 11:12*
Endless, speculating on   *1 Tim. 1:4*

Generosity (See also Beneficence, Liberality)
Of God   *Ps. 103:3-12*
Command regarding   *Matt. 5:42*
Example of   *Prov. 31:20*

Gentile (See also Foreigner, Jew)
Guilty of sin   *Rom. 2:14-15*
Salvation available to   *Rom. 1:16*
Paul, an apostle to   *Acts 21:19*
Message of salvation preached to   *Acts 28:28*
Became fellow members of church   *Eph. 3:6*
No distinction between Jew and   *Gal. 3:28*

Gentleness (See Humility, Kindness, Tolerance)
Of Christ   *2 Cor. 10:1*
Deal with others in spirit of   *1 Cor. 4:21*
Restoring fellow-believers in spirit of   *Gal. 6:1*
A characteristic God likes   *1 Pet. 3:4*

Gethsemane
Garden of Christ's agony   *Matt. 26:36; Luke 22:39*

Gideon
Angel appeared to   *Judg. 6:11*

Lord called to deliver Israel   *Judg. 6:14*
Replaced Baal altar with one to the Lord   *Judg. 6:26–27*
Prayed for signs of assurance   *Judg. 6:36–40*
Delivered Israelites from Midianites   *Judg. 8:22*
Declined being king   *Judg. 8:23*
Faith of   *Heb. 11:32*

Gift (See Calling, Generosity)

■ Of eternal life:
  From God   *John 3:16*
  In Christ   *Rom. 6:23*
Of Holy Spirit   *Luke 11:13*
Of faith   *Eph. 2:8*
Given to each believer   *1 Cor. 12:4–11*
Comes from Father   *James 1:17*
Good stewards of   *1 Pet. 4:10*

Gilead

Land granted to Reubenites   *Num. 32:1–30*
Invaded by Ammonites   *Judg. 10:17*

Gilgal

Joshua camped there   *Josh. 4:19; 9:6*
Saul made king there   *1 Sam. 10:8; 11:14*
Saul sacrificed there   *1 Sam. 13:8; 15:12*

Glory (See also Majesty, Presence of God)

Of God   *Exod. 24:15–17; 40:34; Luke 2:9; Acts 7:55*
Of Christ   *John 12:41; 17:5; Luke 9:32; 1 Tim. 3:16*
Of temporal things   *Matt. 4:8; 1 Thess. 2:6; 1 Pet. 1:24*
■ Of believers:
  By the Spirit   *2 Cor. 3:18*
  By Christ's work   *Heb. 2:9–10*
  Greatness of   *Rom. 8:18*
■ Of God's, reflected:
  In Christ   *John 1:14*
  In man   *1 Cor. 11:7*

Gluttony
Warned against   *Prov. 23:1–3*
Attribute of the wicked   *Phil. 3:19*
Leads to poverty   *Prov. 23:21*
Jesus accused of   *Matt. 11:19*

God (See also Jesus Christ, Holy Spirit)
- Characteristics of:
  Omnipotence   *Jer. 32:17, 27*
  Omnipresence   *Ps. 139:7–12*
  Omniscience   *Amos 9:2–3*
  Foreknowledge   *Isa. 48:3–5*
- Moral Characteristics of:
  Impartiality   *1 Pet. 1:17*
  Love   *1 John 4:8*
  Mercy   *Lam. 3:22–23*
  Holiness   *Rev. 4:8*
  Justice   *Ps. 89:14*
- Manifestations of:
  Voice of   *Deut. 5:22–26*
  Glory of   *Exod. 40:34–35*
  In Jesus   *John 14:9*

God the Father (See God)

Godliness (See also Holiness, Righteousness)
Response to grace   *Titus 2:11–12*
Value of   *1 Tim. 4:8*
As our aim   *1 Tim. 6:11*
Wrong view of   *1 Tim. 6:5*
A supplement of faith   *2 Pet. 1:5–6*

Gold (See also Money)
As money   *Ezra 8:25–28; Ezek. 7:19*
Utensils made of   *Exod. 25:26, 29, 38, 39*
Figurative   *Prov. 17:3; Jer. 51:7; 1 Cor. 3:12*
Symbolic   *Dan. 2:32–45; Rev. 21:18–21*

Golden Rule
Given by Jesus   *Matt. 7:12; Luke 6:31*

Gomorrah (See also Sodom)
Judged   *Gen. 18:20; 19:24, 28; Isa. 1:9; Matt. 10:15*

Good News (See also Gospel, Evangelism)
As refreshment   *Prov. 15:30; 25:25*
Preached by Paul   *Acts 14:15*

Goodness (See also Righteousness, Virture)
- Of God:
  To all   *Ps. 145:9*
  Abundance of   *Ps. 31:19*
  Rejoicing in   *Exod. 18:9; 2 Chron. 6:41*
  Satisfied with   *Jer. 31:14*
- Given to those who:
  Fear God   *Ps. 31:19*
  Continue in his grace   *Rom. 11:22*

Goshen
Allotted to Israelites in Egypt   *Gen. 45:10; 46:34; 47:4*
No plagues there   *Exod. 8:22; 9:26*
Region in Canaan   *Josh. 10:41; 11:16*

Gospel (See also Evangelism, Good News, Preaching, Witnessing)
Of God   *Rom. 1:1*
Of Christ   *2 Cor. 2:12*
God's power   *Rom. 1:16*
- Source of:
  Hope   *Col. 1:23*
  Faith   *Acts 15:7*
  Salvation   *2 Thess. 2:13-14*
- Preaching of:
  To the whole creation   *Mark 16:15*
  By Jesus   *Mark 1:14-15*

Gossip (See also Backbiting, Slander)
Forbidden under law   *Lev. 19:16*
Consequences of   *Prov. 16:28*
Result of idleness   *1 Tim. 5:13*

Government (See also Kingdom, Politics, Society)
Christ's reign   *Isa. 9:6-7*
■ Christians to:
  Obey   *Rom. 13:1-7*
  Pray for   *1 Tim. 2:1-3*

Grace (See also Mercy)
■ The source of:
  Justification   *Rom. 3:24*
  Faith   *Acts 18:27*
  Salvation   *Acts 15:11*
  Forgiveness   *Eph. 1:7*
■ Descriptions of:
  Sufficient   *2 Cor. 12:9*
  Glorious   *Eph. 1:6*
  Rich   *Eph. 2:7*

Gratitude (See Thankfulness, Ingratitude)

Greed (See also Avarice, Covetousness)
Attributed to false teachers   *2 Pet. 2:14*
■ Results in:
  Betrayal   *Luke 22:1-6*
  Trouble   *Prov. 15:27*
  Murder   *1 Kings 21:1-16*
■ Qualities of:
  Never satisfied   *Eccles. 1:8; 5:10*
  Exploits   *2 Pet. 2:3*

Grief (See also Comfort, Mourning, Sorrow)
- Attributed to:
  Holy Spirit   *Eph. 4:30*
  Suffering servant   *Isa. 53:3*
  Jesus   *Mark 3:5*
- Results from:
  Hardness of heart   *Mark 3:5*
  Death   *2 Sam. 19:1–2*
  Disease   *Job 2:11–13*
  Rebelliousness   *Isa. 63:10*

Growth (See also Disciple, Holiness, Sanctification)
In grace and knowledge of Christ   *2 Pet. 3:18*
In Christ-likeness   *Eph. 4:13*
In Christ   *Eph. 4:15*
Of Jesus in wisdom   *Luke 2:52*

Guidance (See also Decision, Will of God)
Continuing   *Isa. 58:11*
By God   *Ps. 48:14; 73:24*
Need of   *Prov. 11:14*
By the Holy Spirit   *Acts 16:6–10*

Guilt (See also Conviction of Sin, Remorse, Shame)
A result of sin   *Exod. 20:7*
Leads to restoration   *Lev. 6:4*
Of uncleanness   *Lev. 5:2*
Of all shown through the Law   *Rom. 3:19*

H
Habakkuk
Prophet of God   *Hab. 1:1*
Questions of   *Hab. 1:2-3, 12-13, 17*
Prayer of   *Hab. 3:1-19*

Hagar
Mother of Ishmael   *Gen. 16:3*
Comforted by angel   *Gen. 16:10*
Allegory of   *Gal. 4:24*

Haggai
Prophet of God   *Hag. 1:1*
Urged rebuilding of the temple   *Hag. 1:1-15*
Rebuked the priests and people   *Hag. 2:11-14*

Hair (See also Beard)
Covering of   *1 Cor. 11:6-7*
Cutting of   *Lev. 19:27; 1 Cor. 11:14-15*
Of a Nazirite   *Num. 6:5*
■ Figurative of:
Many   *Ps. 40:12*
Respect   *Prov. 16:31*
Complete destruction   *Isa. 7:20*

Ham
Son of Noah, cursed   *Gen. 9:18, 22*
His descendants   *Gen. 10:6; 1 Chron. 1:8; Ps. 105:23*

Haman
Official under Xerxes   *Esther 3:1-2*
His sin and fall   *Esther 3:3-10; 7:1-10*

Hand (See also Anthropomorphism)
Laying on of   *Acts 6:6; 8:18; 1 Tim. 4:14*
Lifting of   *Ps. 28:2; 63:4*

H

■ God's hand symbolic of:

Omnipotence   *Ps. 17:7; 20:6; 44:3*

Miracles   *Exod. 3:20*

Protection   *Ps. 139:10*

Provision   *Ps. 145:16*

Punishment   *Ps. 75:8*

Handicapped (See also Lameness)

Jesus healed the blind man   *John 9:1–11*

Paul healed the cripple   *Acts 14:8–10*

God will protect the crippled   *Ezek. 34:16*

Hannah

Mother of Samuel   *1 Sam. 1:11–19*

Her song   *1 Sam. 2:1–10*

Happiness (See also Contentment, Joy)

■ Of the wicked:

Short lived   *Job 20:5*

Unstable   *Luke 20:20*

Temporary   *Luke 16:24–25*

■ Obtained through:

Trusting God   *Prov. 16:20*

Fearing God   *Ps. 128:1–2*

Obeying God   *John 13:15–17*

Harp (See also Music)

■ Used:

To drive out evil spirits   *1 Sam. 16:16–23*

In worship   *Ps. 33:2*

To entertain   *Gen. 31:27*

By the wicked   *Isa. 5:11–12*

In the temple orchestra   *1 Chron. 16:5*

By the prophets   *1 Sam. 10:5*

Harvest (See also Agriculture, Feast)

Feast of   *Exod. 23:16*

Joy of   *Isa. 9:3*

- Figurative of:
  Judgment   *Jer. 51:33; Hos. 6:11*
  People needing God   *Jer. 8:20; Matt. 9:37–38*
  World's end   *Matt. 13:30, 39*
  Final judgment   *Rev. 14:15*

Hatred (See also Anger, Malice)

A work of the flesh   *Gal. 5:20*
Liable to judgment   *Matt. 5:22*
- Recipients of:
  God   *Exod. 20:5*
  Christ   *John 15:25*
  Believers   *Matt. 5:11; 24:9*
  Evil doers   *Ps. 26:5*

Head (See also Body)

- Figurative of:
  God   *1 Cor. 11:3*
  Christ   *Eph. 1:22*
  Man   *1 Cor. 11:3, 7*
  Pride   *Ps. 83:2*
  Confidence   *Luke 21:28*
  Joy   *Ps. 23:5*

Health (See also Disease, Medicine, Sickness)

- Detriments to:
  Sin   *Ps. 38:3*
  Wickedness   *Ps. 55:23*
  Immorality   *Prov. 7:22–27*
- Aids to:
  Obedience   *Prov. 4:20–22*
  Food   *Acts 27:34*
  Exercise   *1 Tim. 4:8*

Heart (See also Soul)

- Source of:
  Actions   *Matt. 12:33–35*

    Desires   *Rom. 10:1*
    Obedience   *Rom. 6:17*
    Sorrow   *John 14:1*
- Conditions of:
    Pure   *Ps. 73:1*
    Contrite   *Ps. 51:17*
    Proud   *Jer. 49:16*
    Hardened   *Rom. 2:5*
    Believing   *Rom. 10:10*
    Loving   *Matt. 22:37*
    Trusting   *Prov. 3:5*

Heaven (See also Unbeliever)

God rules over   *Ps. 47:7-8*
God's goodness to   *Acts 14:17*
Are guilty before God   *Rom. 1:18-19*
God wants them to be saved   *Titus 2:11*
Not to be imitated   *Jer. 10:2-3; Matt. 6:7-8*
Declaring God's glory among   *Ps. 96:3*

Heaven (See also Eternity, Hell, Paradise)

- Characteristics of:
    No corruption   *1 Cor. 15:42, 50*
    No pain   *Rev. 21:4*
    No death   *Luke 20:36*
    Joy   *Luke 15:7*
    Peace   *Luke 16:25*
    Glory   *Rom 8:17-18*
- Residents of:
    God   *1 Kings 8:30*
    Christ   *Heb. 9:12, 24*
    Righteous   *Matt. 25:34-37*
    Angels   *Matt. 18:10*

Hebron

Joshua conquered it   *Josh. 10:36*
Capital under David   *2 Sam. 2:1; 3:2; 5:1*

Heir (See also Birthright, Firstborn, Inheritance)
Christ   *Heb. 1:2*
By promise   *Gal. 3:29*
By faith   *Rom. 4:13–14*
Through God   *Gal. 4:7*
- The recipient of:
  Kingdom   *James 2:5*
  Salvation   *Heb. 1:14*
  Eternal life   *Titus 3:7*
  Promise   *Heb. 11:9*

Hell (See also Eternity, Second Death, Sheol)
- Everlasting:
  Fire   *Matt. 25:41*
  Punishment   *Matt. 25:46*
  Destruction   *2 Thess. 1:9*
- Residents of:
  Devil   *Matt. 25:41*
  Fallen angels   *2 Pet. 2:4*
  Disobedient   *Rom. 2:8–9*
  Beast and false prophet   *Rev. 19:20*

Heresy (See also Apostasy)
How to recognize   *2 John 9–11*
Avoiding fellowship with   *Gal. 1:7–9*
Warning to teachers of   *Titus 3:10–11*

Hermon, Mount
East of Jordan   *Josh. 12:1–5*

Herod
The Great   *Luke 1:5*
- Antipas:
  Tetrarch of Galilee and Perea   *Luke 3:1*
  Imprisoned John the Baptist   *Matt. 14:1–12*
  Had John beheaded   *Mark 6:22–28*
  Pilate sent Jesus to   *Luke 23:7–11*

- Agrippa I:
  Killed James   *Acts 12:1–2*
  Imprisoned Peter   *Acts 12:3–11*
  Death of   *Acts 12:20–23*
- Agrippa II:
  Paul's defense before   *Acts 26:1–23*
  Rejection of the gospel   *Acts 26:27–29*

Herodias

Wife of Herod's brother Philip   *Mark 6:17*
Planned death of John the Baptist   *Matt. 14:1–10;
     Mark 6:14–29*

Hezekiah

Life of extended   *2 Kings 20:1–11*
Pride of   *2 Kings 20:12–19*
Death of   *2 Kings 20:21*
Carried out reforms in the temple   *2 Chron. 29:3–36*
Prospered   *2 Chron. 31:20–21*

Hiram

King of Tyre   *2 Sam. 5:11; 1 Kings 10:11*
Brass-worker to Solomon   *1 Kings 7:13*

History

Spiritual lessons from   *1 Cor. 10:1–11; Heb. 4:1–2*
Accuracy of the Word's   *2 Tim. 3:16*

Holiness (See also Consecration, Godliness,
     Sanctification)

Christian's responsibility   *Eph. 4:22–24; 1 Pet. 1:15*
Call to   *Rom. 12:1*
Comes through grace   *Titus 2:11–12*
Possessed by Christ   *Luke 1:35; Acts 4:27*
Attained by the discipline of God   *Heb. 12:10*

Holy Place (See Sanctuary, Tabernacle)

Holy Spirit (See also Comforter, Fruit of the Spirit)

- Characteristics of:
  Omniscience   *1 Cor. 2:10*
  Omnipresence   *Ps. 139:7*
  Teaches   *John 14:26*
  Comforts   *Acts 9:31*
  Can be grieved   *Eph. 4:30*
  Convicts men   *John 16:8-11*
  Fills believers   *Acts 2:4*
  Gives power to believers   *Acts 1:8*
  Gives guidance   *Acts 16:6-10*

Home (See also Hospitality)

Witnessing to people at   *Luke 8:39*
Prophet not honored there   *Mark 6:4*
Hospitality in   *Acts 16:15*
Church in   *Philem. 1:1-2*
Sharing of   *John 19:27*
- Figurative:
  As human body   *2 Cor. 5:6*
  Where Holy Spirit lives   *John 14:23*
  Eternal   *2 Cor. 5:1*

Homosexuality (See also Sexual Conduct)

Condemned   *Gen. 19:1-11, 24; Lev. 18:22; Rom. 1:26-27*

Honesty (See also Lying, Sincerity, Truthfulness)

Blessing of   *Isa. 33:15-16*
In all things   *Heb. 13:18*
Pleases God   *Ps. 15:1-2*

Honor (See also Respect, Reverence)

- Should be given to:
  Parents   *Exod. 20:12; Eph. 6:2*
  God   *1 Tim. 1:17*

84

Widows   *1 Tim. 5:3*
Christ   *John 5:23*
- Shown by:
Giving to God first   *Prov. 3:9*
Accompanies wisdom   *Prov. 3:13–16*
Follows humility   *Prov. 15:33*

Hope (See also Anchor, Spiritual; Assurance; Confidence)

- Characteristics of:
Blessed   *Titus 2:13*
Sure   *Heb. 6:19*
Good   *2 Thess. 2:16*
- Of the Christian towards:
God   *Ps. 39:7*
Christ   *1 Cor. 15:19*
Salvation   *Rom. 5:1–5*
- Inspires:
Purity   *1 John 3:3*
Courage   *Rom. 5:4–5*
Joy   *Rom. 12:12*
Assurance   *Heb. 6:18–19*

Horeb, Mount

Name for Mount Sinai   *Exod. 3:1; 17:6; 33:6; Deut. 1:6; 4:10*
Law given there   *Deut. 4:10–14*

Horse

- Symbolic of:
Stubbornness   *Ps. 32:9*
Poor judgment   *Jer. 8:6*
Trust   *Hos. 14:3*
- Uses:
In war   *Exod. 14:9*
For travel   *Deut. 17:16*
In idolatry   *2 Kings 23:11*

Hosea

Called by the Lord   *Hos. 1:1*

Married to unfaithful wife   *Hos. 1:2-3*

Marriage illustrates Israel's unfaithfulness   *Hos 4–5*

Hospitality (See also Benevolence, Home)

A Christian practice   *Rom. 12:13*

A quality of a bishop   *1 Tim. 3:2*

A test of discipleship   *Matt. 25:35*

Should be done willingly   *1 Pet. 4:9*

■ Shown by:

Washing of feet   *Luke 7:44*

Kissing   *Luke 7:45*

Providing food and housing   *Luke 11:5-8*

Humility (See also Meekness, Modesty, Pride)

Of Christ   *Matt. 11:29*

God teaches   *Deut. 8:3*

Needed to receive grace   *James 4:6*

God is with those who have   *Isa. 57:15*

Of a child   *Matt. 18:4*

Husband (See also Bridegroom, Marriage, Wife)

Sanctified by his wife   *1 Cor. 7:16*

Head of his wife   *1 Cor. 11:3*

■ Responsibility to wife:

Be faithful   *Mal. 2:14-15*

Instruct   *1 Cor. 14:34-35*

Love   *Eph. 5:25-33*

Live with   *Matt. 19:3-9*

Provide for   *1 Tim. 5:8*

Hymn (See also Music, Song)

■ Used for:

Joyful expressions   *Matt. 26:30*

Edification   *Eph. 5:19; 1 Cor. 14:15*

Worshiping God   *2 Chron. 23:18*

- Inspired by:
  Victories   *Judg. 5:1–31*
  Deliverance   *Exod. 15:1–19*
  Answered prayer   *1 Sam. 2:1–10*
  Joy   *Luke 1:46–56*

Hypocrisy (See also Honesty, Integrity)

Ascribed to Pharisees and scribes   *Matt. 23:13–15*
Pharisee's leaven is symbolic of   *Luke 12:1*
- Description of:
  Deceptive lives   *Ezek. 33:31–32*
  Unclean hearts   *Luke 11:39*
  Blindness   *Matt. 23:17–26*
  Seeks self-acclaim   *Matt. 6:2–5*

I

Idolatry (See also Abomination, Baal)
- Results in:
  Bondage   *Gal. 4:8–9*
  Degradation   *Rom. 1:22–23*
- Condemnation of:
  Making images   *Exod. 20:4; Lev. 26:1*
  Serving   *Exod. 20:5; Ps. 81:9*

Ignorance (See also Knowledge, Wisdom)
Sin because of   *Acts 3:17*
In former state   *1 Pet. 1:14*
Of the Scriptures   *Matt. 22:29*
Due to hardness of heart   *Eph. 4:18*
From choice   *2 Pet. 3:5*

Immorality (See also Lust, Morality, Sin)
Condemned   *1 Cor. 6:9*
No repentance for   *1 Cor. 5:1*
Characterized by sexual perversion   *Rom. 1:24–32*

Immortality (See also Death, Eternity, Life)
Through Jesus   *John 3:15; 2 Tim. 1:10*
Given to those who are patient in well doing   *Rom. 2:7*
Victory over death   *1 Cor. 15:53–54*
Ascribed to God   *1 Tim. 1:17*
Of the righteous   *Matt. 25:46*
Gift of God   *Rom. 6:23*
Promise of   *1 John 2:25*

Impatience (See also Intolerance, Patience)
Dealing with   *Rom. 5:3–4; Eph. 4:1–3*
Of Moses   *Numbers 20:7–12*
Of Martha at death of Lazarus   *John 11:20–21*
Of Jesus' mother at the wedding   *John 2:3*
Of Jesus' parents in the temple   *Luke 2:48–49*

Incarnation (See also Birth, Nativity)

Purpose of   *John 1:9-14*
Spirits confess truth of   *1 John 4:2*
Foretold   *John 7:42*
Timing of   *Gal. 4:4*

Incense (See also Offering, Sacrifice, Temple)

■ Offering of:
  By priests   *Lev. 16:12-13*
  Exclusively for God   *Exod. 30:37-38*
■ Symbolic of:
  Prayer   *Rev. 5:8*
  Christ's intermediacy   *Rev. 8:3-4*
  Praise   *Mal. 1:11*

Incest (See also Family, Sexual Conduct)

Forbidden   *Lev. 18:6-18*
Punishments for   *Lev. 20:11-20; Deut. 27:20-23*

Ingratitude (See also Thankfulness)

Remembered   *Deut. 25:17-19*
Condemnation of   *2 Chron. 32:25*
■ Causes of:
  Opulence   *Deut. 6:10-12*
  Self-sufficiency   *Deut. 8:12-18*
  Pride   *Dan. 5:18-20*
  Negligence   *Luke 17:12-18*

Inheritance (See also Birthright, Heir)

By faith   *Gal. 3:18-22*
Incorruptible   *1 Pet. 1:4*
In Christ   *Eph. 1:11-12*
■ Of the believers:
  Eternal life   *Matt. 19:29*
  Blessings   *1 Pet. 3:9*
  Kingdom of God   *Matt. 25:34*
  Honor   *Prov. 3:35*

Injustice (See also Justice, Law, Righteousness)
Those who practice it shall perish   *Prov. 11:7*
Command to avoid   *Lev. 19:15*
The Lord avenges   *1 Thess. 4:6*

Insanity
Sent as judgment from God   *Deut. 28:28*
Feigned by David   *1 Sam. 21:13–15*
Jesus accused of   *Mark 3:21*

Insomnia (See also Sleep)
Of the rich   *Eccles. 5:12*
Promise to claim regarding   *Prov. 3:24*

Inspiration (See also Revelation)
Of Scripture   *2 Tim. 3:16; Heb. 1:1; 2 Pet. 1:21*
By a voice   *Acts 8:29*
By a vision   *Ezek. 11:24*
By a dream   *Dan. 7:1*

Instability (See also Change, Faithfulness, Steadfastness)
In service   *Matt. 6:24*
In faith   *James 1:7–8*
From disobedience   *Matt. 7:26–27*

Instruction (See also Teacher)
By priests   *Lev. 10:11*
By the Word   *2 Tim. 3:16*
From nature   *Matt. 6:25–30*
By prophets   *Heb. 1:1*
By object lessons   *Jer. 27:2–11; 28; Ezek. 4:1–3*

Integrity (See also Character, Honesty, Sincerity)
As protection   *Ps. 25:21*
As guide   *Prov. 11:3*
In trials   *Job 2:9*

Intercession (See also Mediator, Prayer, Substitution)

Of Christ for believers   *Heb. 7:25*
By the Holy Spirit for believers   *Rom. 8:26-27*

Intolerance (See also Bigotry, Tolerance)

Not to be a part of the Christian life   *Eph. 4:1-3*

Isaac (See also Rebecca)

Named by God   *Gen. 17:19*
Born to Sarah in her old age   *Gen. 17:15-16*
Descendants of are children of promise   *Rom. 9:7-12*
Married to Rebecca   *Gen. 24:63-67*

Isaiah

Prophet during reigns of four kings   *Isa. 1:1*
Foretold punishment of Jews for idolatry   *Isa. 2:6-20*
Foretold the coming of Messiah   *Isa. 9:1-7*
Prophesied judgments on other nations   *Isa. 10:5-34*
Promised restoration of the Jews   *Isa. 43:1-13*
Foretold conversion of the Gentiles   *Isa. 45:5-25*

Ishmael

Son of Abraham   *Gen. 16:11*
Promises concerning   *Gen. 16:11-12; 17:20*
Sent away by Abraham   *Gen. 21:6-21*

Israel (See also Jacob)

New name of Jacob   *Gen. 32:28*
Name given to descendants of   *Gen. 43:32*
What God required of   *Deut. 10:12-22*
Administered by judges   *Judg. 2:16-19*
■ Administered by kings:
   Saul   *1 Sam. 8:22; 10:1; 11:15; 13:1*
   David   *2 Sam. 5:3-4*
   Solomon   *1 Kings 1:38-39*
Final conversion of   *Rom. 11:26-27*

J

Jacob

Son of Isaac and brother of Esau   *Gen. 25:24-26*
Cheated brother out of blessing   *Gen. 27:1-29*
Father of twelve sons   *Gen. 35:22*
Father of Joseph   *37:2*

Jael

Israelite heroine   *Judg. 4:17; 5:24*

Jairus

Jewish leader whose daughter was brought back to life
    Matt. 9:18; Mark 5:22; Luke 8:41

James, Son of Alphaeus

Christ appeared to after resurrection   *1 Cor. 15:7*
Spoke on behalf of Gentile converts   *Acts 15:14-21*
Wrote epistle   *James 1:1*

James, Son of Zebedee

An apostle   *Matt. 4:21-22*
Fisherman and brother of John   *Luke 5:10*
Present at Transfiguration   *Matt. 17:1*
Martyred   *Acts 12:2*

Japheth

Son of Noah   *Gen. 9:27*

Jason

Persecuted at Thessalonica   *Acts 17:5; Rom. 16:21*

Jealousy (See also Covetousness, Envy)

■ In man:
  Makes him furious   *Prov. 6:34*
  Causes strife   *1 Cor. 3:3*
■ Example of: Joseph's brothers   *Gen. 37:4*

Jehoahaz
Son of Jehu, king of Israel   *2 Kings 10:35; 13:4*
Evil king of Judah   *2 Kings 23:31; 2 Chron. 36:1*

Jehoiachin
Evil king of Judah defeated and taken captive
    2 Chron. 36:8–10

Jehoiada
High priest killed Athaliah, restoring Jehoash
    2 Kings 11:4
Repaired the temple   *2 Kings 12:7*
Abolished idolatry   *2 Chron. 23:16*

Jehoiakim
Evil king of Judah taken captive   *2 Kings 23:34–24:1;*
    2 Chron. 36:4–8; Dan. 1:2

Jehoram
Son of Jehoshaphat, king of Judah   *1 Kings 22:50*
(Joram) Son of Ahab, king of Israel   *2 Kings 1:17*

Jehoshaphat
Good king of Judah   *1 Kings 15:24*

Jehu
Son of Hanani   *1 Kings 16:1; 2 Chron. 19:2*
Son of Nimshi, king of Israel   *1 Kings 19:16; 2 Kings 9:1*

Jephthah
Judge of Israel   *Judg. 11:1–34*

Jereboam (See also Rehoboam)
Rebelled against King Solomon   *1 Kings 11:26*
Fled to Egypt to escape Solomon   *1 Kings 11:40*
First king of Israel after the revolt   *1 Kings 12:20*
Instituted idol worship   *1 Kings 12:28–29*

Jeremiah
Priest and Prophet   *Jer. 1:1*
Called by the Lord   *Jer. 1:4-19*
Sent letter at prophecy to exiles   *Jer. 29:1-32*
Persecuted for prophesying   *Jer. 20:1-2*

Jericho
Called City of Palm Trees   *Deut. 34:3*
Besieged by Joshua seven days   *Josh. 6:1-16*
Walls fell at trumpet blast and shouts   *Josh. 6:20*
Where Jesus healed blind man   *Matt. 20:29-34*

Jerusalem (See also Zion)
Called City of the Great King   *Ps. 48:2*
Captial of David's kingdom   *1 Kings 15:4*
Feasts of Jews held at   *Ezek. 36:38*
Prayer center of Israelites   *1 Kings 8:37-39*
Ark brought to   *2 Sam. 6:12-19*
Temple built in   *2 Chron. 3:1*
Captured by king of Babylon   *2 Chron 36:17-20*
Rebuilt walls of   *Neh. 2:20; 7:1*
Gospel first preached in   *Luke 24:47*

Jesse
David's father   *Ruth 4:17-22*
His posterity   *1 Chron. 2:13*

Jesus Christ (See also Christ)
Pre-existence of   *John 8:58*
Deity of   *Rom. 9:5; Col. 2:9*
Wisdom of   *1 Cor. 1:30; Col. 2:3*
Subordinate to Father   *John 5:19; 14:28*
Creator   *John 1:2-3; Col. 1:15-16*
Incarnation   *Matt. 1:18-21; John 1:1-18*
Teaching   *Matt. 5-7, 13*
Miracles   *Matt. 14:13-21; 23-29; Luke 7:13-15*
Death of   *Matt. 27:31-54; John 19:17-30*

Resurrection   *John 20:11–18*
Ascension   *Acts 1:9–11*
As way of salvation   *John 14:6; Acts 4:12*
Second Adam   *Rom. 5:12–21; 1 Cor. 15:22–45*
Image of God   *Col. 1:15*
Author of faith and grace   *Heb. 12:12; 2 Cor. 12:9*
Redeemer   *1 Cor. 1:30; Gal. 3:13; Col. 1:14*
And the Law   *Matt. 5:17–19; Rom. 10:14*
Sinlessness   *2 Cor. 5:21*
Significance of his death   *Col. 2:14–15*
Faith in him   *Rom. 3:26; 10:13; John 1:12; John 3:23*
Union with him   *Gal. 2:16–20; Col. 2:11–13*
Return   *John 14:3; 1 Thess. 4:16; 5:1–11*
Judge   *2 Cor. 5:10; 2 Tim. 2:4*
Lord   *Phil. 2:9–11*
Sustainer of Christians   *Jude 24*
High priest for Christians   *Heb. 7:15–10:20*

Jethro
Moses' father-in-law   *Exod. 18:12*

Jewelry
Brought as an offering   *Exod. 35:22*
Used by kings as symbol of authority   *Esther 8:1–2*

Joab
Nephew of David   *2 Sam. 8:16*
Killed Abner   *2 Sam. 3:23*
Killed Absolom   *2 Sam. 18:14*
Joined Adonijah's usurpation   *1 Kings 1:7*

Joash
(Jehoash) King of Israel   *2 Kings 13:10*
King of Judah   *2 Kings 11:4; 2 Chron. 23:1–24:23*

Job
Afflicted by Satan   *Job 1:6–2:6*
Patience of in trial   *Job 1:21*

Questioned his plight   *Job 10:1-7*
Tried to vindicate himself   *Job 23:10-12; 27:1-6*
Answered by God   *Job 38:1-41:34*

Joel
Foretold judgments   *Joel 2:1-11*
Foretold giving of God's Spirit   *Joel 2:28-29*

John, Apostle
With Jesus in Gethsemane   *Mark 14:33*
Called pillar of the church   *Gal. 2:9*
Took care of Jesus' mother   *John 19:26*
Called the disciple whom Jesus loved   *John 13:23*
Wrote of his revelation on Patmos   *Rev. 1:9-11*

John the Baptist (See also Elisabeth)
Birth foretold by angel   *Luke 1:11-13*
Preached the coming of Jesus   *Mark 1:7*
Witnessed that Jesus was deity   *John 1:29-34*
Baptized Jesus   *Mark 1:9-10*
Preached repentance and baptism   *Matt. 3:6*
Imprisoned and beheaded by Herod   *Matt. 14:1-12*

Jonah
Prophet of God   *Jon. 1:1*
Disobeyed God   *Jon. 1:2-3*
Swallowed by large fish   *Jon. 1:17*
Delivered from   *Jon. 2:10*
Obeyed God   *Jon. 3:1-5*

Jonathan
Son of Saul   *1 Sam. 13:2*
His love for David   *1 Sam. 18:1*
Killed by Philistines   *1 Sam. 31:2*

Joppa
Tabitha raised from dead there   *Acts 9:36*
Peter lived there   *Acts 10:5; 11:5*

Jordan, River
Miraculously separated for crossing   *Josh. 3:14–16*
Naaman washed in to heal leprosy   *2 Kings 5:10–14*
Jesus baptized in   *Matt. 3:13*

Joseph
Favorite son of Jacob   *Gen. 37:3*
Sold to Egypt by brothers   *Gen. 37:27*
Interpreted dreams   *Gen. 40:5–23; 41:1–37*
Named to prepare for famine   *Gen. 41:39–40, 48–49*
Forgave and helped his brothers   *Gen. 45:1–15*

Joshua
Pleaded with Israelites to go to Canaan   *Num. 14:5–9*
Succeeded Moses   *Num. 27:18–23*
Led people to Canaan   *Josh. 1–4*
Besieged and took Jericho   *Josh. 6*
Challenged Israelites to serve God   *Josh. 24:14–15*

Josiah
King of Judah   *2 Kings 22:1–23:9*

Jotham
King of Judah   *2 Kings 15:32*

Joy (See also Happiness, Victory)
Of the Lord   *Neh. 8:10*
■ Occasions for:
In believing   *Isa. 12:3; Rom. 15:13*
In the Holy Spirit   *Rom. 14:17*
Because of what God has done   *Ps. 92:4*
When a sinner repents   *Luke 15:10*
In trials   *James 1:2*

Jubilee, Year of
Description   *Lev. 25:10, 28; 27:17*
Symbolic   *Isa. 61:2; Luke 4:19*

Judah (See also Israel)
One of tribes of Israel   *Gen. 49:8–12, 28*
Led in occupation of Canaan   *Judg. 1:1–2*
David, king of   *2 Sam. 5:5*
Remained loyal to David in revolts   *2 Sam. 20:1–2*

Judas
Apostle   *Luke 6:16 (also Jude, Thaddeus)*

Judas Iscariot
Disciple who betrayed Jesus   *Matt. 10:4; 26:14, 47*

Judges of Israel
Provided by God   *Judg. 2:16, 18*
People would not listen to   *Judg. 2:17*
■ Instances of corrupt:
  Eli's sons   *1 Sam. 2:12*
  Samuel's sons   *1 Sam. 8:1–3*

Judgment (See also Condemnation, Punishment)
■ Of God:
  Will come to all   *Acts 17:31; 1 Cor. 4:5*
  Administered by Christ   *2 Cor. 5:10*
  Description of   *Matt. 25:31–46; 1 Thess. 1:5–10*
  Comes after death   *Heb. 9:27*

Justice (See also Courts, Mercy, Righteousness)
Of God   *Ps. 75:1–10; Ezek. 18:25*
Lack of   *Isa. 59:14; Mic. 7:3; John 7:24*
Need for   *Prov. 24:23; Isa. 1:17; Zech. 8:16*
God loves   *Ps. 37:28*

Justification (See Atonement, Justice, Righteousness)
Not by the Law   *Rom. 3:20; Gal. 3:11*
By faith   *Acts 13:39; Rom. 1:17*
By works   *James 2:14–26*

K
Kadesh Barnea
Where Israelites murmured against Moses and Aaron
   Num. 13:26; 14:1-45

Keturah
Abraham's second wife   *Gen. 25:1-4*

Key
Symbol of authority   *Matt. 16:19; Rev. 1:18*
Of David   *Rev. 3:7*

Kidron
Brook crossed by David   *2 Sam. 15:23*
Idols destroyed there   *1 Kings 15:13; 2 Kings 23:6*
Frequented by Jesus   *John 18:1*

Kindness (See also Benevolence, Love, Tolerance)
Of the Lord   *1 Pet. 2:3*
In speech   *Prov. 31:26*
In ministry   *2 Cor. 6:6*
Among believers   *Eph. 4:32; Col. 3:12*
To those in need   *1 John 3:17*
To all   *Gal. 6:10*

King (See also Authority)
Israelites asked for a   *1 Sam. 8:4-5*
Israelites rejected God as   *1 Sam. 8:7; 10:19*
Samuel warns about life under a   *1 Sam. 8:10-18*
Saul was first   *1 Sam. 9:27-10:1*
Chosen by divine appointment   *1 Sam. 16:1-13*
God as   *Ps. 24:7; 1 Tim. 1:17*

Kingdom (See also Heaven, Zion)
Of God   *1 Chron. 29:11; Ps. 22:28*
Of Christ   *Matt. 16:28; 2 Pet. 1:11*

Of heaven *Matt. 7:21; 25:1*
Of the world *Rev. 11:15*

Kiriath (Kirjath) Jearim
Where Ark rested for 20 years *1 Sam. 7:2*

Kissing
As greeting in early church *Rom. 16:16; 1 Cor. 16:20*

Kneeling (See also Humility, Prayer)
In prayer *2 Chron. 6:13*
Stephen, during his stoning *Acts 7:59–60*
Before God *Eph. 3:14*
Ezra, in shame for his people *Neh. 9:5–6*

Knowledge (See also Learning, Philosophy, Wisdom)
Of God *Prov. 3:20*
Of Christ *Phil. 3:8*
Of salvation *Luke 1:77*
Gift of *1 Cor. 12:8*
Is pleasant *Prov. 2:10*
More valuable than gold *Prov. 8:10*

L

Laban
Gave Jacob his two daughters   *Gen. 29:1–30*
Envied and oppressed Jacob   *Gen. 30:27; 31:1*
Covenant with Jacob   *Gen. 31:43–55*

Lamb (See also Offering)
Of God   *John 1:29*
As an offering   *Exod. 29:38*
- Figurative:
  Of Christ   *Rev. 5:12*
  Of believers   *John 21:15*

Lamech
Father of Noah   *Gen. 5:25, 29*

Lameness (See also Handicapped, Health)
Healed   *Matt. 11:5; Luke 7:22; Acts 3:2–8*

Lamp (See also Light)
God's Word is a   *Ps. 119:105*
A father's commandment is a   *Prov. 6:23*
- Figurative of:
  Eye is   *Luke 11:34*
  Of the wicked   *Prov. 13:9*

Language (See also Mouth, Speech)
Gift of, by Holy Spirit   *Acts 2:4*
One, on earth   *Gen. 11:1*
More than one, after Babel   *Gen. 11:7–9*

Laodicea
Paul's letter to   *Col. 2:1; 4:16*
Christ's message to the church there   *Rev. 3:14–22*

Laughter
A time for   *Eccles. 3:4*
Of Israel   *Ps. 126:2*

Law (See also Courts, Justice, Ten Commandments)
Of the Lord   *Ps. 19:7*
Given through Moses   *Exod. 20*
All of it must be obeyed   *Gal. 3:10*
No one justified by it   *Rom. 3:20*
Saved from curse of   *Gal. 3:13*
Christ is end of the   *Rom. 10:4*

Lazarus
■ Brother of Mary and Martha:
  Illness of   *John 11:1-4*
  Death of   *John 11:14*
  Raised from the dead   *John 11:38-44*
Parable of the beggar   *Luke 16:19-31*

Leadership (See also Authority, Head, Minister)
By those who don't know the way   *Matt. 15:13-14*
Of God   *Ps. 23:2-3; 37:23; Exod. 20:2*
■ Instances of:
  Moses   *Exod. 6:13; 14:13-14, 21*
  Deborah   *Judg. 4:4-15*

Leah
Wife of Jacob   *Gen. 29:16, 31; 30:17; 31:4; 33:2*

Learning (See also Knowledge, Wisdom)
Need to increase in   *Prov. 1:5*
With God's help   *Dan. 1:17*
Testing authority in   *John 7:17*

Lebanon
Cedars from, used to build Temple   *1 Kings 5:6-18*

Levi
Son of Jacob   *Gen. 29:34*
Avenged his sister Dinah's defilement   *Gen. 34:1-31*

Liberality (See also Generosity)
- Object of:
  Poor   *Deut. 15:11*
  All men   *Gal. 6:10*
- Purpose of:
  Demonstrating one's faith   *James 2:14-16*
  Securing true riches   *1 Tim. 6:17-19*
- Blessings of:
  Honored by Christ   *Matt. 25:40*
  Rewarded   *Prov. 3:9-10*

Liberty
Christians called to   *Gal. 5:13*
Christian law of   *James 1:25*
Not causing offense   *Rom. 14:13-23*
Walk in   *Ps. 119:44-45*
Proclaimed by Jesus   *Luke 4:16-21; John 8:31-36*

Life (See also Immortality)
- Natural:
  Brevity of   *Ps. 90:9-10*
  Put Kingdom of God first in   *Matt. 6:25-33*
  Given up for Christ   *Matt. 10:39*
- Spiritual:
  Source of   *John 14:6*
  Described   *John 3:3-8*
  Evidence of   *1 John 3:14*
  Eternal   *John 3:15*

Light (See also Darkness, Lamp)
- Descriptive of:
  God   *1 John 1:5*
  Jesus Christ   *John 8:12*

Christians   *Matt. 5:14*
God's Word   *Ps. 119:105*
Christian life   *1 John 1:7; 2:9-10*

Lion

King of animals   *Prov. 30:30*
■ Used figuratively of:
Tribe of Judah   *Gen. 49:9*
Jesus Christ   *Rev. 5:5*
Devil   *1 Pet. 5:8*
Antichrist   *Rev. 13:2*

Locusts (See also Pestilence)

Used as a judgment   *Exod. 10:12-19; Deut. 28:38, 42*
Used for food   *Matt. 3:4*

Lois

Grandmother of Timothy   *2 Tim. 1:5*

Loneliness (See also Comfort)

■ Instances of:
Joseph   *Gen. 43:30*
Jeremiah   *Jer. 15:17*
Jesus   *Matt. 26:36-45*
Paul   *2 Tim. 4:16*

Longevity (See also Old Age, Youth)

Allotted years   *Ps. 90:10*
■ Increased by:
Fearing the Lord   *Prov. 9:10-11; 10:27*
Wisdom   *Prov. 3:13, 16*
Honoring parents   *Eph. 6:1-3*

Long-suffering (See also Patience, Tolerance)

Descriptive of God's character   *2 Pet. 3:9*
Exemplified by the prophets   *James 5:10*
Produced by the Spirit   *Gal. 5:22*

To characterize believers   *Eph. 4:1-2*
Needed by pastors   *2 Tim. 4:1-2*

Lord
■ Title applied to:
  God   *Gen. 3:8-9, 14; Lev. 19:2*
  Jesus Christ   *Luke 6:46; Acts 1:21; Rev. 22:20*
Confessing that Jesus is   *Rom. 10:9; Phil. 2:11*

Lord's Day (See also Sabbath)
First day of week   *John 20:1, 19*
Breaking bread on   *Acts 20:7*
The Lord spoke to John on   *Rev. 1:10*

Lord's Prayer (See also Prayer)
Taught to disciples   *Matt. 6:9-13; Luke 11:1-4*
Believers using as example   *Matt. 6:9*

Lord's Supper (See also Communion, Eucharist)
Instituted by Christ   *Matt. 26:26-29*
Observed by early church   *Acts 2:42, 46*
Instructions concerning   *1 Cor. 11:23-34*
Commemorative of Christ's death   *Luke 22:19-20*

Lot
Abraham's nephew   *Gen. 13:10*
Saved from Sodom   *Gen. 19:1-26*

Love (See also Affection, Altruism, Kindness)
Towards God commanded   *Deut. 6:5*
Towards neighbor commanded   *Matt. 22:39*
Exemplified by Christ   *John 15:13*
To be shown among believers   *John 15:12*
Obedience as proof of   *John 14:15*
Defined   *1 Cor. 13:4-7*
Importance of   *1 Cor. 13:1-3, 8-13*
Of the world condemned   *1 John 2:15-17*

Loyalty (See also Character, Faithfulness)
Urged as fitting   *Prov. 24:21; Rom. 13:1-2; Titus 3:1*
Displayed by disciples   *John 6:67-69*
Promised to believers by Jesus   *Heb. 13:5*
Part of God's character   *Deut. 7:9*

Lucifer (See also Satan)
A name of Satan   *Isa. 14:12-14*

Luke
Doctor and companion to Paul   *Col. 4:14; 2 Tim. 4:11*

Lust (See also Adultery, Fornication, Immorality)
Originating in man's heart   *Matt. 15:19*
Christ provided an escape from   *2 Pet. 1:4*
Leads to sin   *James 1:14-15*
Turning away from   *2 Tim. 2:22*
Part of unbeliever's life   *Eph. 2:3*

Lydia
First convert in Philippi   *Acts 16:13-15*

Lying (See also Accusation, False; Deceit; Dishonesty)
Counted as an abomination   *Prov. 6:16-19*
Prayer for deliverance from   *Ps. 120:2*
Originating with the devil   *John 8:44*
Denial that Jesus is the Christ   *1 John 2:21-23*
Associated with disobedience   *1 John 2:4*
The wicked take pleasure in   *Ps. 62:4*

Lystra
Where Paul healed cripple, was worshiped, then
   stoned   *Acts 14:8-20*

M

Macedonia
Paul's mission there   *Acts 16:9*
Generosity of   *2 Cor. 8:1-5*

Magic (See also Astrology, Occult, Witchcraft)
Condemned by law   *Lev. 20:27*
Those practicing judged   *Rev. 21:8*
Failed to drive out demon   *Acts 19:13-16*
Those who had practiced   *Acts 19:19*

Magician (See also Magic)
Condemned by law   *Lev. 20:27*
Helpless in plagues   *Exod. 8:18*
Believed and was baptized   *Acts 8:13, 18-24*

Majesty (See also Glory, King, Presence of God)
■ Of God:
    Glory of   *Isa. 2:19*
    Clothed with   *Ps. 93:1*
■ Of Christ:
    Foretold   *Mic. 5:2-4*
    Witnessed   *2 Pet. 1:16-17*

Malachi
Prophet of God   *Mal. 1:1*
Described sins of the priests   *Mal. 1:6-14*
Described sins of the people   *Mal. 3:6-9, 13-15*
Foretold coming of Elijah and Christ   *Mal. 3:1-3; 4:5-6*

Malchus
High priest's servant whose ear was cut off   *John 18:10*

Malice (See also Evil, Sin)
Comes from perverted heart   *Prov. 6:14, 18-19*
Christians to rid themselves of   *1 Cor. 5:7-8; Eph. 4:31*

Mammon
Worship of   *Matt. 6:24 (KJV)*

Man (See also Woman)
Created for God's glory   *Isa. 43:7*
Created by God   *Gen. 1:26–27*
Made in God's image   *Gen. 9:6*
Wonderfully made   *Ps. 139:13–16*
Sin entered through disobedience   *Gen. 3:1–7*
By one, sin came into the world   *Rom. 5:12*
Continues eternally   *Matt. 25:46*
Parity with others before God   *Prov. 22:2*

Manasseh
■ Son of Joseph:
   Firstborn   *Gen. 41:51*
   His blessing and inheritance   *Gen. 48:1–20*
Evil king of Judah   *2 Kings 21:1–18*

Manna (See also Bread)
Supplied by God   *Exod. 16:4, 15; John 6:31–32*
Despised by people   *Num. 11:4–6*

Marah
Where bitter water was made sweet   *Exod. 15:23*

Mark (John Mark)
Cousin of Barnabas   *Col. 4:10*
Accompanied Paul and Barnabas   *Acts 13:5*
Left Paul and Barnabas   *Acts 13:13*
Paul and Barnabas argue over   *Acts 15:37–40*
Comforted Paul in prison   *Col. 4:10*

Marriage (See also Adultery, Bride, Polygamy)
Instituted by God   *Gen 2:18–24*
Honorable for all   *Heb. 13:4*
Intimate and permanent bond   *Matt. 19:5–6*

M

Dissolved by death   *Rom. 7:2-3*
Means of preventing immorality   *1 Cor. 7:2-4*
- Figurative of:
  God's union with Israel   *Isa. 54:5*
  Christ's union with his church   *Eph. 5:23-32*

Martha
Sister of Mary   *Luke 10:38*
Sister of Lazarus   *John 11:1, 17-27*

Martyrdom
Not to be feared   *Matt. 10:28*
To be accepted if necessary   *Acts 21:13*
- Examples of:
  John the Baptist   *Mark 6:18-29*
  Stephen   *Acts 7:58-60*
  Heroes of faith   *Heb. 11:35-37*

Mary
Mother of Jesus, wife of Joseph   *Matt. 1:1-16*
Observed Jesus' first miracle   *John 2:1-10*
Was present at crucifixion   *John 19:25-26*
Cared for by the disciple   *John 19:27*

Mary Magdalene
Delivered of demons by Jesus   *Luke 8:2*
Helped Jesus and disciples   *Luke 1:1-3*
Was present at crucifixion   *John 19:25*
Was first to see Jesus after resurrection
    John 20:14-18

Matthew
Apostle   *Matt. 9:9 (Also called Levi)*
Sent out   *Matt. 10:3; Acts 1:13*

Mediator (See also Jesus Christ)
- Christ as:
  Between God and man   *1 Tim. 2:5*

Of a new covenant   *Heb. 8:6; 9:15*
A continuing high priest   *Heb. 7:24*
Intercessor   *1 John 2:1*

Medicine (See also Health, Physician, Sickness)
Cheerful heart as   *Prov. 17:22*
Insufficient remedy   *Isa. 1:6*
Used by Good Samaritan   *Luke 10:34*

Meditation (See also Prayer)
On God's Word   *Ps. 119:97-99*
On God's law   *Ps. 1:2*
On God's work   *Ps. 77:12*
For understanding   *Ps. 49:3*

Meekness (See also Humility, Submission)
Serving in spirit of   *James 3:13*
Among the fruits of the spirit   *Gal. 5:22-23*
Characteristic of Christ   *Matt. 11:29; 27:12-14*

Melchizedek
King of Salem who blessed Abraham   *Gen. 14:18*
His priesthood   *Ps. 110:4; Heb. 5:6, 10; 6:20; 7:1*

Mephibosheth
Lame son of Jonathan   *2 Sam. 4:4*
Cherished and spared by David   *2 Sam. 9:1; 21:7*

Mercy (See also Forgiveness, Grace)
Characteristic of God   *Lam. 3:22-23*
To characterize believers   *Matt. 5:7; Luke 6:36*
God showed in salvation   *Titus 3:4-5*
Underlies hope of eternal life   *Jude 21*

Meshach (See also Abednego)
His faith, suffering, and deliverance with Shadrach and
    Abednego   *Dan. 1:1-7; 3:1-30*

Messiah (See also Jesus Christ, Anointed One)
Promised as seed of Abraham   *Gal. 3:16*
Descended from tribe of Judah   *Gen. 49:10*
A king of David's lineage   *Jer. 23:5; Luke 1:32-33*
Described as Son of Man   *Dan. 7:13-14; Mark 8:38*
Preached the Good News   *Isa. 61:1-3; Luke 4:17-19*
Jesus confirmed that he was   *John 13:19*
Paul preached that Jesus was   *Acts 17:2-3*

Methuselah
Oldest man who lived   *Gen. 5:27*

Micah
Prophet of God   *Mic. 1:1*
Told of God's anger   *Mic. 1:2-16*
Described the sin of Israel, Judah   *Mic. 2:1-2, 3:1-12*
Told of Messiah's coming   *Mic. 5:2-4*

Michael
Archangel   *Jude 9; Rev. 12:7*

Michal
David's wife   *1 Sam. 18:20*
Mocks his religious dancing, rebuked   *2 Sam. 6:16, 20*

Midian
Where Moses fled after killing Egyptian   *Exod. 1:11-22*

Milk (See also Food)
■ Figurative:
  Spiritual food   *1 Pet. 2:2*
  Food for new believers   *1 Cor. 3:2*
  Food for immature believers   *Heb. 5:11-14*

Millennium
Described   *Rev. 20:1-6*

Mind (See also Heart, Soul, Will)

Loving God with   Matt. 22:37
Of Christ in believers   Phil. 2:5; 1 Cor. 2:16
Renewal of in believers   Rom. 12:2
Of unregenerate is hostile   Col. 1:21
Unity of   Phil. 2:1–2
Spirit-controlled brings peace   Rom. 8:6
Humble   1 Pet. 3:8

Minister (See also Pastor, Servant)

Example of Christ   Mark 10:45
■ Should be:
  Able to teach   1 Tim. 3:2
  Courageous   Acts 20:22–24
  Diligent   1 Cor. 15:10
  Faithful   1 Cor. 4:2
  Meek   Gal. 6:1
  Prayerful   Acts 6:4
  Filled with Holy Spirit   Acts 1:8
  An example in talk and behavior   1 Tim. 4:12

Ministry (See also Minister, Servant)

Of angels   Ps. 103:20
As servanthood   Matt. 20:22–27
Of God's messengers   1 Cor. 3:5
■ Examples of:
  Preaching the gospel   1 Cor. 1:17
  Building up the church   John 21:15–17; Eph. 4:12
  Praying for others   Col. 1:9
  Teaching   2 Tim. 2:2
  Comforting the distressed   2 Cor. 1:4–6

Miracle (See also Sign)

■ Attributed to:
  God's power   Acts 15:12
  Christ's power   John 2:11
  Spirit's power   Matt. 12:28

To reveal God's glory   *John 11:40*
To reveal Christ's glory   *John 2:11*
Recorded to produce faith   *John 20:30–31*

Miriam

Sister of Moses and Aaron   *Exod. 15:20*
Song of   *Exod. 15:20–21*
Murmured against Moses   *Num. 12:1–2; 10, 15*

Mission (See also Evangelism)

- Of Christ:
    To do God's will   *John 6:38*
    To save the lost   *Luke 19:10*
    To reveal God   *Heb. 1:1–3*
    To fulfil the law   *Matt. 5:17*
    To give his life   *Mark 10:45*
- Of Christians:
    To make disciples   *Matt. 28:16–20*

Missionary

Commission of   *Mark 16:15; 28:19*
Witness of   *1 Chron. 16:23–24*
Message of   *Matt. 24:14; Luke 24:47–48*

Mizpah

Jacob and Laban met there   *Gen. 31:49*
Where Israel sacrificed, fasted and defeated Philistines
    1 Sam. 7:5–11

Moab

Son of Lot and his daughter   *Gen. 19:36–37*
His descendants and territory   *Deut. 2:9, 18; 34:5*

Mocking

- Objects of:
    God   *2 Kings 19:4; Gal. 6:7*
    Christ   *Luke 23:11, 36; Matt. 27:29*
    Believers   *Heb. 11:36*

Modesty (See also Humility, Pride)
Encouraged in dress   *1 Tim. 2:9; 1 Pet. 3:3-4*

Molech
God to whom Canaanites sacrificed their children
   Lev. 18:21; 2 Kings 23:10

Money (See also Commerce, Finances, Riches)
Not to be loaned for interest   *Lev. 25:37; Deut. 23:19*
Love of, a root of evil   *1 Tim. 6:10*
Given as an offering   *Deut. 14:22-29*
Associated with greed   *2 Kings 5:19-27*
Used to pay taxes   *Matt. 17:24-27; 22:17-21*
Used to repair temple   *2 Kings 12:13-14*

Morality/Morals (See also Behavior, Conduct)
Ruined by bad company   *1 Cor. 15:33*
Required by God's Law   *Deut. 11:1*
Taught by Jesus   *Matt. 5:17-48; 6:22-24; 7:7-12*
Preached by prophets   *Isa. 1:17*

Mordecai
Revealed plot against Ahasuerus   *Esther 2:21-23*
Plot against him thwarted by Esther   *Esther 3:1-7:10*

Mortality (See also Death, Immortality)
Consequence of sin   *Rom. 5:12*
Death a common experience   *Heb. 9:27*
End of earthly life   *Eccles. 9:10*
All to be raised from death   *Acts 24:15*
A return to dust   *Gen. 3:19*

Moses (See also Commandment, Exodus, Law)
Descendant of Levi   *Exod. 2:1*
Instructed in Egyptian wisdom   *Acts 7:22*
Refused Egyptian sonship   *Heb. 11:24-27*
Called by God   *Exod. 3:1-10*

Conflict with Pharaoh   *Exod. 7–12*
Commanded to institute the Passover   *Exod. 12:1–29*
Received the Law   *Exod. 20–23*
Sent spies to Canaan   *Num. 13:1–33*
Sinned in anger   *Num. 20:1–13*
Commissioned Joshua   *Num. 27:12–23*
Died in full strength at 120   *Deut. 34:5–7*

Motherhood (See also Fatherhood)
Object of prayer   *Gen. 25:21*
Makes joyful   *Ps. 113:9*
Painful yet joyful   *John 16:21*

Motive (See also Desire)
Ascribed to God   *Ps. 106:8; Ezek. 36:21–22, 32*
Right, required   *Matt. 6:1–18*
Sinful, illustrated by Cain   *1 John 3:12*

Mountain
■ Significant Old Testament events on:
Ark's resting place   *Gen. 8:4*
Giving of the Law   *Exod. 19:2*
Combat with Baal priests   *1 Kings 18:19–40*
■ In Christ's life, place of:
Temptation   *Matt. 4:8*
Sermon   *Matt. 5:1*
Prayer   *Matt. 14:23*
Transfiguration   *Matt. 17:1*
Ascension   *Luke 24:50*

Mourning (See also Bereavement, Sorrow)
■ Caused by:
Death   *Gen. 23:2*
Disobedience   *Ezra 9:3–7*
Desolation   *Joel 1:8–10*
Depravity   *Prov. 5:11*
Transformed into joy and gladness   *Isa. 51:11; 61:3*

Mouth (See also Conversation, Speech, Tongue)

Make all words acceptable   *Ps. 19:14*
Guard carefully   *Ps. 39:1; 141:3*
May the talk of be helpful   *Eph. 4:29*
Keep foul language from   *Col. 3:8*

Murder (See also Death, Hatred)

An act of the sinful nature   *Matt. 15:19*
Results from hatred   *Matt. 5:21–22*
Guilt determined by witnesses   *Num. 35:30*

Music (See also Hymn, Musical Instrument, Singing)

- Used in:
  Entertainment   *Isa. 5:12*
  Weddings   *Jer. 7:34*
  Funerals   *Matt. 9:18, 23*
  Victory celebrations   *Exod. 15:20–21*
  Praising God   *Heb. 2:12; Rev. 14:2–3*
  Fellowship   *Eph. 5:19; Col. 3:16*

Musical Instruments (See also Harp, Music, Trumpet)

- List of:
  Cymbals   *Ps. 150:5; 1 Cor. 13:1*
  Flute, harp, lyre   *Ps. 150:3; Isa. 5:12; Dan. 3:5, 7, 10*
  Strings   *Ps. 150:4*
  Tambourine   *2 Sam. 6:5; Ps. 150:4; Isa. 5:12*
  Trumpets   *Ps. 150:3; Rev. 18:22*

Mystery (See also Revelation, Secret)

Christ's incarnation   *1 Tim. 3:16*
Nature of Christ   *Col. 2:2*
The indwelling Christ   *Col. 1:26–27*
Communion of all Christians   *Eph. 3:4–9*
Hardening of Israel's heart   *Rom. 11:25*
Resurrection   *1 Cor. 15:51–52*

N

Nahum

Prophet of God   *Nah. 1:1*
Described God's greatness and wrath   *Nah. 1:1-14*
Predicted fall of Nineveh   *Nah. 2:1-13*
Told reasons for its fall   *Nah. 3:1-19*

Name

Value of a good   *Prov. 22:1*
- Of believers:
  Will receive new   *Isa. 62:2; Rev. 3:12*
  Written in heaven   *Luke 10:20*
  Known by Christ   *John 10:3*
  Christ's exalted   *Phil. 2:9-10*

Names for God (See also God, Jesus, Holy Spirit)

Father   *John 12:49*
Most High   *Ps. 83:18*
King of kings and Lord of lords   *1 Tim. 6:15*
Judge   *Judg. 11:27*
Lord   *Ps. 16:2*

Naomi

Ruth's mother-in-law   *Ruth 1:1-22*

Naphtali

Son of Jacob   *Gen. 30:8*
Tribe of Israel   *Judg. 1:33*

Nathan

Prophesied to David   *2 Sam. 7:1-17*
Anointed Solomon king   *1 Kings 1:34*

Nathanael

Called by Jesus   *John 1:44-50*

Nation (See also Kingdom, Patriotism)
Believers constitute a   *1 Pet. 2:9–10*
Abraham father of many   *Gen. 17:4–5*
Exalted by righteousness   *Prov. 14:34*
Israel set apart   *Exod. 19:5–6*
All organically connected   *Acts 17:26*
Gospel preached to every   *Matt. 24:14; Rev. 14:6*
Believers from every   *Rev. 15:9*

Nativity (See also Incarnation)
Of Jesus   *Matt. 1:18–25; Luke 2:1–7*

Nazareth
Boyhood home of Jesus   *Matt. 2:23; Luke 2:39–40*
Obscure town   *John 1:46*
Residents rejected Jesus   *Luke 4:16–30*

Nazirite
By birth   *Judg. 13:5, 7*
By vow   *Num. 6:2*
Requirements of   *Num. 6:2–8*
■ Examples of:
  Samson   *Judg. 16:17*
  Samuel   *1 Sam. 1:11*

Nebuchadnezzar (See also Babylon)
Takes Jerusalem, carries captives to Babylon
  Dan. 1:1–4
Builder of Babylon   *Dan. 4:30*
Instrument of God's judgment   *Jer. 27:8*
Touched with insanity   *Dan. 4:28–37*
Ruler of first of four great kingdoms   *Dan. 2:30–40*

Nehemiah (See also Ezra)
Leader in the postexilic community   *Ezra 2:2*
Son of Hachaliah   *Neh. 1:1*
Cupbearer to Artaxerxes I   *Neh. 1:11*

Allowed to rebuild Jerusalem   *Neh. 2:1-8*
Effects reform among Jews   *Neh. 5:1-19*
Supports Ezra in restoration of worship   *Neh. 8-10*

Neighbor (See also Friendship, Love)
Love towards   *Rom. 13:9-10*
Speak truth to   *Eph. 4:25*
Urged to be   *Luke 10:29-37*
Coveting of, forbidden   *Exod. 20:17*

Nervousness (See Anxiety, Care, Impatience)

Nicodemus
Went to Jesus at night   *John 3:1-21*
Assisted at Christ's burial   *John 19:39*

Night (See also Darkness, Day)
Named by God   *Gen. 1:5*
Jesus prays through   *Luke 6:12*
None in heaven   *Rev. 21:25; 22:5*
Figurative of ignorance and unbelief   *Rom. 13:12;*
     1 Thess. 5:5

Nineveh
Jonah's mission to   *Jonah 1:1; 3:2*
Spared by God after repentance   *John 3:5-10*

Noah (See also Ark, Rainbow)
Son of Lamech   *Gen. 5:28-29*
Father of Shem, Ham, and Japheth   *Gen. 5:32*
Righteous man   *Gen. 6:8-9*
Instructed to build ark   *Gen. 6:14-16*
Saved from flood waters   *Gen. 8:1-17*
Covenant established with   *Gen. 9:1-19*
Died when 950   *Gen. 9:29*

O

Oath (See also Curse, Swearing)
God's confirmation of   *Gen. 26:3*
Taking of   *Neh. 5:12*
Despising of   *Ezek. 16:59*
False   *Zech. 8:17*
Not taking of   *James 5:12*

Obadiah
Prophet to Edom   *Obad. 1:1*
Met Elijah   *1 Kings 18:7*
Hid 100 prophets   *1 Kings 18:4, 13*

Obedience (See also Disobedience, Submission)
To the Covenant   *Exod. 24:7*
To God   *1 Sam. 15:22*
To Christ   *2 Cor. 10:5*
To the gospel   *2 Thess. 1:8; 1 Pet. 4:17*
To the faith   *Acts 6:7*
To parents   *Col. 3:20*
To husbands   *Titus 2:5*

Obligation (See also Duty, Responsibility)
To God   *Rom. 14:12*
To believe   *John 8:24*
To other Christians   *1 John 3:16*
To live righteously   *Mic. 6:8*
To the weak   *Acts 20:35*
To evangelize   *Matt. 9:36–38*

Occult
Not to be practiced   *Lev. 19:26–28, 31*
Called sin   *1 Sam. 15:23*
Listed among works of the flesh   *Gal. 5:20*
■ Practiced by:
  The Babylonians   *Isa. 47:9–13*

Belshazzar   *Dan. 5:7, 15*
False prophets   *Matt. 24:24; Jer. 14:14*
Astrologers   *Jer. 10:2*
■ Persons converted from:
  Simon Magus   *Acts 9:13*
  Many burned their books   *Acts 19:18-19*
To increase before Christ's return   *2 Thess. 2:9-12*

Offering (See also Altar, Sacrifice, Tithe)

Willingly brought   *Exod. 35:29*
Sacrificial   *2 Sam. 24:24; Isa. 53:10*
Of Christ to God   *Eph. 5:2; Heb. 9:14*
In righteousness   *Mal. 3:3*
According to one's ability   *1 Cor. 16:1-2*
Of body to God   *Rom. 12:1*

Oil (See also Anointing, Ordination)

For light   *Exod. 35:14*
Anointed for kingship   *1 Sam. 10:1*
Anointed for healing   *Mark 6:13; James 5:14*
Used in offering   *Lev. 2:1*
■ Figurative of:
  Gladness   *Ps. 45:7*

Ointment (See also Perfume)

Used to anoint Christ   *Mark 14:3-9*
Preparation for burial   *Luke 23:55-56*

Old Age (See also Longevity)

Honor to those of   *Lev. 19:32*
Rejecting advice from those of   *1 Kings 12:8*
Fruitfulness in   *Ps. 92:14*
A crown of glory   *Prov. 16:31*
Live righteously in   *Titus 2:2-3*
In reference to widows   *1 Tim. 5:9-10*

Olive
Used to make oil   *Exod. 27:20*
Trees for Israel   *Deut. 6:11*

Olivet, Mount of Olives
Hill near Jerusalem frequented by Jesus and his
    disciples   *Matt. 21:1; 24:3; Mark 11:1; 13:3;
    Luke 21:37; John 8:1*

Omnipotence of God (See also God)
Belongs to him   *Ps. 62:11*
Beyond understanding   *Job 26:14*
Praise for   *Rev. 19:6*
Nothing too difficult for   *Gen. 18:14*
In virgin birth   *Luke 1:35*
In raising Christ   *Eph. 1:19-20*

Omnipresence of God (See also God)
With an individual   *Gen. 28:15*
No escape from   *Ps. 139:7-10*
Awareness of evil and good   *Prov. 15:3*
In heaven and earth   *Jer. 23:24*
Close to everyone   *Acts 17:27*

Omniscience of God (See also God)
Regarding the heart of man   *Ps. 44:21*
Regarding the words of man   *Ps. 139:4*
Is infinite understanding   *Ps. 147:5*
Sees all   *Heb. 4:13*
Beyond man's understanding   *Rom. 11:33-36*

Onesimus
Former slave of Philemon for whom Paul requested
    freedom   *Philem. 1-21*

Onesiphorus
Came to Paul's aid in Rome   *2 Tim. 1:16-17*

Opportunity (See also Decision)

To do good   *Gal. 6:10*
Making the most of   *Col. 4:5*
For salvation   *2 Cor. 6:2*
For evangelism   *John 4:35*
Used for evil   *Matt. 26:16*
To hear God's voice   *1 Sam. 3:2–10*

Oppression (See also Affliction, Bondage)

Not to be guilty of   *Lev. 25:14*
Deliverance from   *Ps. 72:4*
Commanded to relieve   *Isa. 1:17*
Of poor and needy   *Amos 4:1; 5:11*
By Satan   *Acts 10:38*
Plea for deliverance from   *Ps. 119:134*

Ordination (See also Anointing)

Of a prophet   *Jer. 1:5–10*
Of the disciples   *Mark 3:14*
Of the powers of the state   *Rom. 13:1*
Of a preacher and apostle   *1 Tim. 2:7*
Of elders   *Titus 1:5*

Orphan (See also Adoption)

Not to afflict   *Exod. 22:22*
God helper of   *Ps. 10:14*
Finds mercy   *Hos. 14:3*
God against those who oppress   *Mal. 3:5*
Command to look after   *James 1:27*
Provide food for   *Deut. 14:29*

Overcoming (See also Battle, Victory)

The wicked one   *1 John 2:13*
The world   *John 16:33*
Evil with good   *Rom. 12:21*
The corruption of world   *2 Pet. 2:20*
Rewarded for   *Rev. 2:7, 11, 17, 26; 3:5, 12, 21*

P

Pain (See also Adversity, Affliction, Suffering)
Christ suffered   *Matt. 27:27-31; 45-50*
Paul suffered   *2 Cor. 11:23-29*
Abolition of   *Rev. 21:4*

Parable (See also Allegory)
Listening to   *Ps. 49:4*
Purpose of   *Matt. 13:13-17*
Of the net   *Matt. 13:47-52*
Of mustard seed   *Mark 4:30-32*
Of the sower   *Luke 8:4-15*
Of lost sheep, coin, and son   *Luke 15*

Paradise (See also Heaven)
Promised by Jesus   *Luke 23:43*
One caught up into   *2 Cor. 12:3-4*
Incorruptible inheritance in   *1 Pet. 1:4*
Tree of life in   *Rev. 2:7*
Reward great in   *Luke 6:23*

Pardon (See also Forgiveness, Mercy)
Of sin   *Mic. 7:18*
Prayer for   *Ps. 25:11*
Of one another   *Eph. 4:32*
Refusal to   *Matt. 18:28-35*
Promise of   *Isa. 55:7*
Withheld   *Exod. 23:21*

Parents (See also Family, Motherhood)
To be honored by children   *Exod. 20:12*
To be provided for   *1 Tim. 5:8*
Betrayed by   *Luke 21:16*
To have obedient children   *1 Tim. 3:4*
Grieving   *2 Sam. 18:33*
Providing for children   *2 Cor. 12:14*

Partiality (See also Justice)

Commanded not to show   *1 Tim. 5:21; James 2:1-7*
Not an attribute of wisdom   *James 3:17*
Of parent for child   *Gen. 37:3*
With regard to the poor   *Lev. 19:15*
God does not show   *1 Pet. 1:17*
With regard to salvation   *Gal. 3:26-29*

Passover (See also Feast, Communion)

Institution of   *Exod. 12*
And the Last Supper   *Matt. 26:19; Luke 22:15*
An act of faith   *Heb. 11:28*
Lamb of, type of Christ   *1 Cor. 5:7*

Pastor (See also Elder, Minister)

Given the gift of   *Eph. 4:11*
To be a shepherd   *1 Pet. 5:2-3*
Commanded to preach   *2 Tim. 4:1-2*
To pray and minister   *Acts 6:4*

Patience (See also Impatience, Long-suffering, Waiting)

Waiting for the Lord   *Ps. 130:5*
Produced by tribulation   *Rom. 5:3*
Need of   *Heb. 10:36*
Holy Spirit produces   *Gal. 5:22*
Of God for the unrepentant   *2 Pet. 3:9*

Patriotism (See also Nation, Treason)

Of a centurion   *Luke 7:2-5*
Paul appeals to   *2 Cor. 11:22*

Paul (See also Apostle)

Conversion of   *9:1-19*
Claims apostleship   *Gal. 1:1, 11-12*
Imprisoned for Christ   *Phil. 1:12-13*
Minister of the gospel   *Col. 1:23*

Peace (See also Contentment, Quiet, Rest)
God of   *Phil. 4:9*
With one another   *Mark 9:50*
Fruit of the Spirit   *Gal. 5:22*
Of God   *Phil. 4:7*
Of Christ   *John 14:27*
None for the wicked   *Isa. 57:21*

Peace Offering (See also Offering, Sacrifice)
Sacrifice of   *Lev. 3:1*
Commanded to make   *Exod. 20:24*
To be offered in Canaan   *Deut. 27:1-7*

Peniel
Where Jacob wrestled with the angel   *Gen. 32:30*

Penitence (See also Confession, Remorse)
Prayer of   *Ps. 51*
Joy in heaven over   *Luke 15:7*
God's goodness leads to   *Rom. 2:4*
Godly sorrow brings   *2 Cor. 7:10*
Example of   *Luke 18:9-14*

Pentecost, Day of (See also Holy Spirit)
Coming of Holy Spirit   *Acts 2:1-12*
Amazement on   *Acts 2:5-12*
Peter's sermon on   *Acts 2:14-36*

Perdition (See also Hell, Punishment)
Son of   *John 17:12; 2 Thess. 2:3*
Of ungodly men   *2 Pet. 3:7*

Perfection (See also Sanctification)
Growing toward   *Heb. 6:1*
Prayer for   *2 Cor. 13:9*
Requirements for   *Matt. 19:21*
Limit of   *Ps. 119:96*

Perfume (See also Ointment)
Rejoices the heart   *Prov. 27:9*
Poured upon Christ   *Mark 14:3*
For making incense   *Exod. 30:35*

Persecution (See also Accusation, False; Suffering)
By friends   *Job 19:22*
Deliverance from   *Ps. 7:1-2*
Pray for those guilty of   *Rom. 12:14, 19-21*
Against the church   *Acts 11:19*
Promise of   *2 Tim. 3:12*

Perseverance (See also Long-suffering, Steadfastness)
In chasing the enemy   *Judg. 8:4*
In practicing forgiveness   *Matt. 18:21-22*
Until the end   *Mark 13:13*
In well-doing   *Gal. 6:9*
In prayer   *Eph. 6:18*

Person (See also Man)
No partiality of   *Gal. 2:6*
Of Christ in God's image   *Heb. 1:3*

Pestilence (See also Locust, Plague)
Prayer for deliverance from   *1 Kings 8:37-39*
Not to be feared   *Ps. 91:5-6*
Coming of   *Matt. 24:7*
Sent by God   *Amos 4:10*
Upon the disobedient   *Jer. 42: 21-22*

Peter (See also Apostle, Pentecost)
Brought to Christ and renamed   *John 1:40-42*
Called to be a disciple   *Matt. 4:18-20*
Walked on the water   *Matt. 14:22-33*
Confessed Jesus as Messiah   *Matt. 16:13-17*
Prophecy concerning later role   *Matt.16:18-19*

Rebuked   *Matt. 16:21–23*
Failed to understand Christ   *John 13:7–11*
Denied knowing Jesus   *Matt. 26:69–75*
Witnessed empty tomb   *John 20:1–9*
Preached at Pentecost   *Acts 2:14–41*
Healed a beggar   *Acts 3:1–10*
Leader in early church   *Acts 5:1–16; 15:7–14*
Ministry to Gentiles   *Acts 10:1–11:18*
Rebuked by Paul   *Gal. 2:11–21*
Commended Paul   *2 Pet. 3:15–16*

Pharaoh (See also Egypt)
King of Egypt   *Gen. 41:46*
Dream of interpreted by Joseph   *Gen. 41:25–36*
Named Joseph a ruler   *Gen. 41:39–41*

Pharisees (See also Sadducees, Sanhedrin)
At John's baptism   *Matt. 3:7–8*
Questioning Jesus   *Mark 7:5*
Attitude toward tax collectors   *Luke 5:30*
Believers who were   *Acts 15:5*

Philemon
Slave owner of Onesimus   *Philem. 1–25*

Philip (See also Apostle)
Listed as an apostle   *Matt. 10:3*
Called by Christ   *John 1:43*
Preached in Samaria   *Acts 8:5–6*
Witnessed to official   *Acts 8:26–39*

Philippi
Paul persecuted there   *Acts 16:12*
Paul's letter to church   *Phil. 1:1–4:23*

Philistines (See also David, Joshua)
Abimelech, king of   *Gen. 26:8*

Captured Samson   *Judg. 16:21*
Captured the ark of God   *1 Sam. 5:1–2*
Fought against Israel   *1 Chron. 10:1*
Lord will destroy   *Jer. 47:4*

Philosophy (See also Knowledge, Wisdom)
Schools of Greek   *Acts 17:18*
Warning against deceptive   *Col. 2:8*
Not enough for salvation   *1 Cor. 1:20–25; 2:6–10*

Physician (See also Health, Medicine)
Luke, the beloved   *Col. 4:14*
No help from   *Mark 5:26*
For those who are sick   *Mark 2:17*

Pilate
Pontius, governor of Judah   *Luke 3:1*
Examined Jesus   *Matt. 27:1–2, 11–26*

Pillar
Of salt   *Gen. 19:26*
Of cloud and fire   *Exod. 13:21*
Of the temple   *1 Kings 7:13–22*
■ Figurative:
   Of the church   *1 Tim. 3:15*
   Of leaders of the church   *Gal. 2:9*

Pity (See also Compassion, Sympathy)
Upon the poor   *Prov. 19:17*
For one another   *1 Pet. 3:8*
Of God for his people   *Joel 2:18*

Plague (See also Pestilence)
Against the Egyptians   *Exod. 9:14; 11:1*
Of leprosy   *Lev. 13:2*
Protection from   *Ps. 91:10*
Figurative of death   *Hos. 13:14*

Plan of Salvation (See also Salvation)
Need for   *Rom. 3:9–12, 23*
God made known his   *Luke 2:8–11; John 3:16–17*
Christ made possible the   *Rom. 5:6; 1 Pet. 2:24*
Summary of   *1 Cor. 15:3–8; 1 Tim. 3:16*

Pleasure (See also Amusement, Sensuality)
At God's right hand   *Ps. 16:11*
Of the rich condemned   *James 5:5*
Of creation to God   *Rev. 4:11*
Wicked approve of   *Rom. 1:32*
In unrighteousness   *2 Thess. 2:12*

Poetry (See also Art)
■ Illustrations of:
  A psalm of praise   *Ps. 136*
  Song of Mary   *Luke 1:46–55*
  Song of the angels   *Luke 2:14*

Politics (See also Alliance, Compromise, Government)
Of convenience   *Luke 23:12*
For gain   *Acts 24:26*
Bribery in   *1 Sam. 8:3*
Crooked   *Acts 25:7–9*

Polygamy (See also Marriage)
In Cain's line   *Gen. 4:23*
David's   *2 Sam. 5:13*
Solomon's   *1 Kings 11:1–3*

Poor People (See also Charity, Justice, Welfare)
Protection of   *Isa. 14:30*
Blessings on   *Luke 6:20*
Provision for   *Ps. 68:10*
The righteous understand   *Prov. 29:7*
Among believers   *Rev. 2:9*

Possessions (See Money, Property, Prosperity)

Potiphar
Joseph's master in Egypt   *Gen. 39:1-6*
His wife's attempt to seduce Joseph   *Gen. 39:6-20*

Pottery
Molding of   *Jer. 18:3-4*
Making, symbol of God's creative work   *Isa. 64:8*
Breaking, symbol of God's judgment   *Jer. 19:10-11*

Poverty (See also Beggar, Riches)
■ Can result from:
   Too much sleep   *Prov. 20:13; 24:33*
   Too much drinking or eating   *Prov. 23:21*

Power (See also Omnipotence, Strength)
Spirit to give   *Acts 1:8*
Spirit of   *2 Tim. 1:7*
God gives to the weak   *Isa. 40:29*
Of God   *1 Chron. 29:11*
Of Christ   *Matt. 28:18*
Over the enemy   *Luke 10:19*

Praise (See also Prayer, Thanksgiving, Worship)
■ To God:
   Because He is worthy   *2 Sam. 22:4; Eph. 1:6*
   In manner of living   *Eph. 1:12*
   Continually   *Heb. 13:15*
   Angels singing   *Luke 2:13-14*
   With instruments   *Ps. 150*
Of self   *Prov. 27:2*

Prayer (See also Intercession, Lord's Prayer, Worship)
Plea for God's attention   *Ps. 64:1*
Of the righteous   *Prov. 15:29*
Of faith   *James 5:15*

For forgiveness   *Ps. 51:1–9*
Continuing in   *Col. 4:2*
Hindrance to   *1 Pet. 3:7*
Of Christ   *John 17*

Preaching (See also Pastor, Sermon, Teaching)
Entrusted to man by God   *Titus 1:2–3*
Power of God in   *1 Cor. 1:18*
Of the disciples   *Luke 9:6*
About Christ's death   *1 Cor. 1:23*
To all the world   *Luke 24:47*
Of Peter   *Acts 2:14–36*
Of Paul   *Acts 13:16–41*

Predestination (See also Election)
According to God's purpose   *Rom. 8:28–30*
According to his will   *Eph. 1:11*
Of Christ's death   *Acts 2:23*

Pregnancy (See also Baby)
God forms unborn child   *Ps. 139:13–16*
Of Eve, the first to conceive   *Gen. 4:1*
Of Sarah in her old age   *Gen. 21:1–2*
Of Elizabeth in her old age   *Luke 1:24, 57*
Of Hannah, who prayed for a son   *1 Sam. 1:11*
Of Mary   *Matt. 1:20–25; Luke 1:31–34*

Presence of God (See also Glory, God, Majesty)
Hiding from   *Gen. 3:8*
Appearance of   *Num. 20:6*
Joy in   *Ps. 16:11*
Coming to with praise   *Ps. 100:1–2*
Brings conviction of sin   *Isa. 6:1–7*

Presumption (See also Arrogance, Disobedience, Pride)
Sins of   *Ps. 19:13*

Ignoring authority   *2 Pet. 2:10*
Sinning purposefully   *Num. 15:30*
A prophet speaking falsely   *Deut. 18:22*

Pride (See also Arrogance, Boasting, Conceit)
Before a fall   *Prov. 16:18*
Origin of   *1 John 2:16*
Deceptiveness of   *Jer. 49:16*
Of the wicked   *Ps. 10:4*
Warning against   *Rom. 12:3*

Priest (See also Aaron, Chief Priest, Priesthood)
■ Jesus as:
  Appointed by God   *Heb. 5:5*
  Appointed forever   *Heb. 5:6*
  Intercessor   *Rom. 8:34*
  Is able to sympathize   *Heb. 4:14*
  He is faithful   *Heb. 2:17*
■ The Christian as:
  Worshiper   *1 Peter. 2:5*
  To God   *Rev. 1:6*
Converted   *Acts 6:7*

Priesthood (See also Aaron, Priest, Offering)
Of Aaron   *Exod. 28:1; Heb. 5:1-5*
Of Melchizedek   *Gen. 14:18; Ps. 110:4*
Of Christ   *Heb. 4:14; 5:5-10; 7:24*
Of believers   *1 Pet. 2:5*

Priscilla
Wife of Aquila, coworker with Paul   *Acts 18:1-3*

Prison (See also Captivity, Liberty, Prisoner)
Satan freed from   *Rev. 20:7*
Paul's witness in   *Eph. 6:20*
Willingness to go to   *Luke 22:33*
Peter freed from   *Acts 12:6-10*

Prisoner (See also Bondage, Prison)
For Christ   *Phil. 1:13–14*
Of hope   *Zech. 9:12*
Lord's promise for   *Isa. 42:7*
Mistreatment of   *Isa. 20:4*

Profanity (See also Blasphemy, Swearing)
Using God's name falsely   *Lev. 19:12; 1 Cor. 12:3*
As blasphemy   *Rom. 2:24; James 2:7*
Not to be practiced   *Col. 3:8; James 3:10; 5:12*
The Law forbids   *Exod. 20:7*

Promise (See also Covenant, Testament, Vow)
Of God   *Titus 1:2; Heb. 10:23*
In Christ   *Eph. 2:13; 3:6*
Of Christ to disciples   *John 14*
Gentiles share in   *Eph. 3:6*

Property (See also Money)
Rich in   *Gen. 30:43*
Coveting   *Luke 12:15–21*

Prophecy (See also Prophet)
Gift of   *Rom. 12:6; 1 Cor. 12:10*
Origin in the Holy Spirit   *2 Pet. 1:21*
To be heeded   *1 Thess. 5:20; 2 Pet. 1:19*
Associated with a vision   *Dan. 9:21–27*

Prophet (See also Prophetess, Revelation)
Appointed by God   *Jer. 1:5–9*
God's instrument   *Hos. 12:13*
Receiving of   *Matt. 10:41*
Without honor at home   *Matt. 13:57*
■ Examples of:
  Moses   *Deut. 34:10*
  Isaiah   *Matt. 3:3; 15:7*
  Ezekiel   *Ezek. 3:4*

Prophetess (See also Prophet)

- Examples of:
  Miriam *Exod. 15:20*
  Deborah *Judg. 4:4*
  Huldah *2 Kings 22:14*
  Anna *Luke 2:36*

Propitiation (See also Atonement, Sacrifice)

Demonstration of God's justice *Rom. 3:25*
Christ dying for sin *1 John 2:2*
Act of God's love *1 John 4:10*

Prosperity (See also Blessing, Riches)

Peril of *Luke 12:13–21*
Basing life on *Ps. 52:6–7*
Of the unrighteous *Ps. 73:12*

Prostitution (See also Lust, Sexual Conduct)

Avoiding *Prov. 5:8; Rom. 13:14; 1 Thess. 4:3*
Leads to hell *Prov. 5:5*

Protection

- Of man by God:
  In time of trouble *Ps. 46:1; Jer. 16:19*
  In time of evil *Jer. 17:17*
  When no one cares *Ps. 142:4*

Proverb (See also Wisdom)

Purpose of *Prov. 1:2–6*
Understanding of *Prov. 1:6*
Solomon's use of many *1 Kings 4:29–32*
Quoted by Jesus *Luke 4:23*

Providence (See also Sovereignty)

For the earth *Gen. 8:22; Matt. 5:45*
For believers *Matt. 6:33; 10:28–31*
For salvation *Luke 2:10–11; 2 Pet. 3:9*

Prudence (See also Acting Wisely, Discretion, Wisdom)

Wisdom dwells with   *Prov. 8:12*
Brings knowledge   *Prov. 14:18*
Involves silence at times   *Amos 5:13*
Solomon's gift of   *2 Chron. 2:12*

Psalms (See also Hymn, Music)

Of encouragement   *Col. 3:16*
Of thanksgiving   *Ps. 95:2*
Of praise   *Ps. 104*
Of prayer   *Ps. 102*
Singing of   *1 Chron. 16:9; James 5:13*

Publican, Tax Collector (See also Taxes)

Jesus eating with   *Matt. 9:11*
Humble prayer of   *Luke 18:13*
Levi   *Luke 5:27*

Punishment (See also Condemnation, Damnation, Wrath)

Of children   *Prov. 13:24; 19:18*
Eternal   *Matt. 25:46; Rev. 20:14-15*
Of evildoers   *1 Pet. 2:14*
Of angels   *Jude 6*

Purification (See also Purity, Washing)

Of leper   *Lev. 14:2*
From sin   *Ps. 51:7*
By the Word   *Ps. 119:11; Eph. 5:26*
By Christ's blood   *1 John 1:7*
Symbolic, of one another   *John 13:5-15*

Purity (See also Chastity, Cleanliness, Sanctification)

Is blessed   *Matt. 5:8*
In a corrupt world   *Phil. 2:14-15*
Think on   *Phil. 4:8*

Q

Quarrel (See also Arguing, Fighting)
Caused by drunkenness *Prov. 23:29–30*
Preventing *Phil. 2:14*
False teachers indulging in *1 Tim. 6:3–5*
Example of *Acts 15:36–39*

Queen (See also King)
Of Sheba *1 Kings 10:1*
Vashti *Esther 1:9*
Esther *Esther 7:2*
Of heaven *Jer. 44:17, 25*
Candace *Acts 8:27*

Quiet (See also Peace)
Better than toil *Eccles. 4:6*
Strength in *Isa. 30:15*
Of the sea *Mark 4:39*
In heaven *Rev. 8:1*
Before the Lord *Hab. 2:20*

Quiet Time (See also Meditation, Prayer)
■ To pray:
  In the Spirit *Eph. 6:18*
  Giving thanks *1 Thess. 5:18*
  With the mind *1 Cor. 14:15*
  For help in temptation *Mark 14:38*
  For forgiveness of sin *1 John 1:9*
■ To praise God:
  For his love and goodness *Ps. 107:1*
  For what he has done *Ps. 111:1-9*
To study his Word *2 Tim. 3:16-17*

R

Rabbi (See also Minister, Teacher)
Christ the true   *Matt. 23:8*
- Term of respect:
  Used by disciples   *John 1:38; 6:25*
  Used by Nicodemus   *John 3:2*

Race
Christian life compared to   *1 Cor. 9:24; Heb. 12:1*
Renewed strength for   *Isa. 40:31*
Patiently running   *Heb. 12:1*

Q

R

Rachel
Daughter of Laban   *Gen. 29:10*
Jacob's love for   *Gen. 29:17-18, 20*
Death of   *Gen. 35:19*
Sons of   *Gen. 35:24*

Racism (See also Bigotry, Intolerance)
Paul speaking against   *Rom. 3:9-10; Gal. 3:28*
Jesus speaking against   *Luke 9:49-50; 18:9-14*
- Instances of:
  By Israelites   *Ps. 65:5*
  By Joshua   *Num. 11:26-29*
  By Pharisees   *Luke 7:39*
  By Samaritans   *John 4:9*
  Early Christians   *Acts 10:45*

Rahab
Harlot who hid Israelite spies   *Josh. 2:1-21; 6:22*
Commended for her faith   *Heb. 11:31; James 2:25*

Rain (See also Cloud)
The Flood   *Gen. 7:12*
Withheld as punishment   *1 Kings 8:35-36; 17:1*
Sent by God   *Job 5:8-10; Matt. 5:45*

Rainbow (See also Noah)
God's promise   *Gen. 9:12-16*
In Ezekiel's vision   *Ezek. 1:28*
Around the throne   *Rev. 4:3*
On an angel's head   *Rev. 10:1*

Ramah
Home of Samuel   *1:19-20; 7:15-17*

Ransom (See also Redemption, Atonement)
Christ's death as   *Mark 10:45; 1 Tim. 2:5-6*

Rape
Death penalty for   *Deut. 22:25-27*
Of Tamar by Amnon   *2 Sam. 13:6-33*
Of Dinah   *Gen. 34:2*

Reasoning (See also Knowledge, Wisdom)
Job and friends   *Job 13:6*
God and the sinner   *Isa. 1:18*
In public praying and speaking   *1 Cor. 14:13-19*
Without considering God   *James 4:13-17*

Rebecca (See also Isaac)
Wife of Isaac   *Gen. 24:67*
Plotting by   *Gen. 27:5-6*
Burial   *Gen. 49:31*

Rebellion (See also Disobedience)
Of Israel against God   *1 Sam. 8:4-9*
Of Saul   *1 Sam. 15:22-23*
Of mankind   *Rom. 1:18-32*
Of angels   *Jude 6*
Of Satan   *Isa. 14:12-15*

Reconciliation (See also Fellowship)
To brother   *Matt. 5:23-24; 18:15-17*

To God by Christ's death   *Rom. 5:10–11*
Of whole creation   *Col. 1:19–20*

Red Sea (See also Exodus)
Miraculous parting of   *Exod. 14:21*
Crossing of   *Exod. 14:22*
Destruction of Egyptians in   *Exod. 14:26–28*

Redeemer (See also Jesus Christ, Redemption)
Job's faith in   *Job 19:25*
David's prayer to   *Ps. 19:14*
Is strong   *Jer. 50:34*
Of Israel   *Isa. 49:7*
Defends orphans   *Prov. 23:1*

Redemption (See also Cross, Ransom)
In Christ Jesus   *Rom. 3:24*
Christ our   *1 Cor. 1:30; Eph. 1:17; 4:30*
Sent by God   *Ps. 111:9*
Of all creation   *Rom. 8:19–23*

Regeneration (See also Conversion, Salvation)
Spiritual rebirth   *Titus 3:5*
Produces new nature   *Col. 3:10*
By the Word of God   *1 Pet. 1:23*
Required   *John 3:3*

Rehoboam
King of Judah   *1 Kings 11:43–12:1; 14:21–31*
His conflict with Jereboam   *1 King 12:1–19; 14:30*

Rejoicing (See also Happiness, Joy)
■ Because of:
  God's salvation   *Rom. 15:13*
  God's creation   *Isa. 65:18*
  Jesus' birth   *Matt. 2:10*
  The repentance of sinners   *Luke 15:7*
  Hope in Christ   *Rom. 12:12*

Relationship (See also Behavior, Family, Friendship)

Of believers as children of God   Rom. 8:16
- Of believers with Christ:
Rooted in Him   Col. 2:7
Fellow heirs with   Rom. 8:17
- Of believers with Holy Spirit:
Indwelt by   Rom. 8:9
Taught by   John 14:26

Of believers with one another   1 Cor. 12:12-14, 26
- Of believers with non-believers:
Not to marry   2 Cor. 6:14-15
To be good examples to   Matt. 5:13
To do good to   Matt. 5:14-16

Religion (See also God, Salvation)

Mystery of   1 Tim. 3:16
Pure   James 1:26-27
- True:
Description of   Matt. 22:36-40; Rom. 10:1-13
Test of   2 Cor. 13:5; 1 John 4:7-21
Consistency of   2 Tim. 4:7
Without power   2 Tim. 3:8

Remnant (See also Israel)

God's grace toward   Isa. 1:9
Prayer for   Isa. 37:4
Deliverance of   Mic. 2:12

Remorse (See also Conviction of Sin, Guilt, Penitence)

- Leads to:
Calling on the Lord   Ps. 41:4
Recognizing sin   Luke 15:18
Confessing sin   Ps. 51:3-4
Coming too late   Heb. 12:17

Renewal (See Revival)

Repentance (See also Conversion, Penitence)
The Lord responds to   2 Chron. 7:14
Requires humility   2 Kings 22:19
In conversion   Acts 3:19
By Christians   Rev. 3:3
Producing fruit   Luke 3:8
Producing joy   Luke 15:7
To be preached   Luke 24:47

Reproof (See also Discipline)
Provides understanding   Prov. 15:32
Results in wisdom   Prov. 29:15
In teaching   2 Tim. 4:2
In Christian love   Rev. 3:19
In discipline   Heb. 12:5

Reputation (See also Character, Integrity)
For wisdom   1 Kings 10:7
For righteousness   Prov. 18:10
For faith   Rom. 1:8
Acceptable before God   Rom. 14:18

Resentment (See Anger, Bitterness, Retaliation)

Respect (See also Honor)
For government   Rom. 13:7
Shown by children   Eph. 6:1-2
Shown by wives   Eph. 5:33
For all   1 Pet. 2:17

Responsibility (See also Duty, Obligation)
To brother   Gen. 4:9
For sin   Jer. 31:30
To work for God   Matt. 9:37
For one's behavior   Rom. 14:12-13

To teach   *2 Tim. 2:2*
To love one another   *1 John 3:16; 4:11*

Rest (See also Peace, Sleep)
- In God:
  By trusting   *Ps. 37:5*
  With confidence   *1 Pet. 1:21*
- In Christ:
  When troubled   *Matt. 11:28*
  For the soul   *Ps. 116:7*
None for the rebellious   *Heb. 3:11*
- From work:
  God initiated   *Exod. 23:12*
  Heavenly   *Rev. 14:13*

Restitution (See also Justice)
Making full   *Exod. 22:5-6, 12*
Made by oppressor   *Job 20:18*
At conversion   *Luke 19:8*

Restoration
Example in Abraham's life   *Gen. 20:14*
Of the Kingdom   *Acts 1:6-8*
Of sinning believer   *Gal. 6:1*
Of the body   *Matt. 12:13; Mark 8:25*

Resurrection (See also Crucifixion)
Of Jesus   *John 20:1-20*
Disciples witness to   *Acts 1:22*
Hope of believers   *Rom. 6:5; 1 Cor. 15:13, 42*
Power experienced   *Phil. 3:10*
Of the righteous dead   *Rev. 20:5-6*

Retaliation (See also Revenge)
With evil prohibited   *Rom. 12:17; 1 Pet. 3:9*

Retarded
Not exempt from heaven   *Matt. 19:13-14*

Reuben
Firstborn of Jacob   *Gen. 29:32*
Inheritance of descendants   *Josh. 13:15-23*

Revelation (See also Inspiration, Mystery, Scripture)
Through prophets   *Deut. 18:18*
All to be known   *Mark 4:22*
Through Jesus   *John 15:15*
By the Spirit   *1 Cor. 2:10; Eph. 3:1-6*

Revenge (See also Retaliation, Vengeance)
Example of   *Gen. 34:1-31*
■ As God's responsibility:
  Against the enemy   *Deut. 32:41; Prov. 20:22*
  Prohibited   *Rom. 12:19*
  Against evil   *Rom. 13:4*

Reverence (See also Awe, Fear, Worship)
Shown to God   *Exod. 3:5*
To God above all   *1 Chron. 16:25; Job 36:26*
Towards Christ   *1 Pet. 3:15*

Revival (See also Holy Spirit)
Accomplished by God   *Ps. 51:10; 80:7*
Through His Word   *Ps. 119:25*
Of the soul   *Ps. 19:7*

Reward (See also Blessing, Judgment)
■ Given for:
  Showing love   *Matt. 10:42*
  Perseverance   *Phil. 3:14; James 1:12*
  Righteousness   *2 Tim. 4:8*
  Suffering   *2 Tim. 2:12*
Given by God   *Matt. 6:6*

Riches (See also Abundance, Money, Poverty)
Source of   *Deut. 8:18*
Abuse of   *Prov. 28:20*
Futility of   *Matt. 6:19; Luke 12:20*
Spiritual   *Acts 3:6; Eph. 3:8*
As a hindrance   *Mark 10:24; Luke 6:24*

Ridicule (See Mocking)

Righteous, The (See also Righteousness)
God   *Ps. 7:11*
Jesus Christ   *1 John 2:1*
Eternal life for   *Matt. 25:46*
God's care over   *1 Pet. 3:12*
Are fruitful   *Ps. 92:12–14*
Afflictions of   *Ps. 34:19*

Righteousness (See also Godliness, Justice, Justification)
Of God   *Rom. 1:17; 3:21*
Of sinners   *Isa. 64:6*
God loves   *Ps. 33:5*
Of Christ   *1 Cor. 1:30*
Persecuted for   *Matt. 5:10*
Kingdom of God is   *Rom. 14:17*
In new heavens and new earth   *2 Pet. 3:13*

River
In the city of God   *Ps. 46:4*
■ Likened to:
  Life   *Ps. 1:3; Rev. 22:1*
  Prosperity   *Isa. 66:12*
  Place of safety   *Isa. 33:21*

Road (See also Way)
The way of the Lord   *Deut. 5:33; 1 Sam. 12:23*
Blessings of walking in the Lord's ways   *Ps. 128:1*

Robbery (See also Thief)
Command against   *Exod. 20:15*
Of the poor   *Prov. 22:22*
Of the Father's house   *Jer. 7:11*
Of neighbors   *Lev. 19:13*
Causes destruction   *John 10:10*

Rock (See also Foundation)
Christ the   *1 Cor. 10:4; 1 Pet. 2:4*
Source of water for Israel   *Isa. 48:21*
Figuratively, of the body of Christ   *1 Pet. 2:5*
House built on   *Matt. 7:24*
Tomb hewn out of   *Mark 15:46*

Roman Empire (See also Rome)
Ruled by Caesars   *Luke 2:1; Phil. 4:21*
Taxed by   *Luke 2:1*
Paul was citizen of   *Acts 22:27-29*
Paul's defense in court of   *Acts 25:10*

Rome (See also Roman Empire)
Paul imprisoned at   *Acts 28:17, 30*
Church of   *Rom. 1:7*
Paul's desire to visit church at   *Rom. 1:10-11*
Paul's desire to preach the gospel at   *Rom. 1:15*

Ruler (See also King, Palace, Throne)
Evil   *Eph. 6:12*
Used in derision   *Acts 7:27*
Ultimately God   *2 Kings 19:15*
Authority given to man   *Gen. 1:26*

Ruth
Widow devoted to mother-in-law   *Ruth 1:16-17, 22*
Gathered grain in Boaz's field   *Deut. 24:19; Ruth 2:2*
Married Boaz   *Ruth 4:13*

S
Sabbath (See also Lord's Day)
Its holiness   *Exod. 20:8*
For rest   *Lev. 16:31*
Blessing in keeping it   *Isa. 56:2*
Profaning of   *Ezek. 22:8*
Jesus is Lord of   *Matt. 12:8*
Made for man   *Mark 2:27*

Sacrifice (See also Altar, Animal, Offering)
Of Christ for sin   *Heb. 9:26*
Love more important than   *Mark 12:33*
Lives acceptable to God   *Rom. 12:1*
Loss for Christ   *Phil. 3:7–8*

Sadducees (See also Pharisees, Sanhedrin)
Tempting Jesus   *Matt. 16:1*
Teaching of   *Matt. 16:11*
Sayings of   *Matt. 16:2*
Against teaching of the resurrection   *Acts 4:1–2; 23:7*

Safety (See Protection, Security)

Saint (See also Holiness, Sanctification)
Called of God   *Rom. 1:7; 1 Cor. 1:2*
Immorality not fitting   *Eph. 5:3*
Any member of God's family   *Eph. 2:19*
God will not forsake   *Ps. 37:28*

Salt
As a seasoning   *Job 6:6*
■ Figurative:
  Of believer   *Matt. 5:13*
  Speech seasoned with   *Col. 4:6*

Salvation (See also Deliverance, Plan of Salvation)
Through Christ   *Gal. 1:4; 2 Tim. 1:9–10*
Gift of God   *John 3:16; Rom. 6:23*
By faith   *Luke 7:50; Eph. 2:8*
Working it out with fear   *Phil. 2:12*
God's plan for   *1 Thess. 5:9–10; 2 Pet. 3:9*
Now is day of   *2 Cor. 6:2*
Completion of   *Rom. 13:11*

Samaria (See also Israel)
Capital of Israel   *1 Kings 16:24–29*
Threatened with judgment   *Isa. 28:1–4*
Churches established in   *Acts 9:31*
Jesus talked with woman of   *John 4:7–30*

Samson (See also Judges of Israel)
Blessed of the Lord at birth   *Judg. 13:24*
Had great strength from God   *Judg. 15:14–15*
Lost his strength   *Judg. 16:15–17, 19*
Imprisoned by his enemies   *Judg. 16:21*
Enabled to avenge his enemies   *Judg. 16:28–30*

Samuel
Son of Elkanah and Hannah   *1 Sam. 1:19, 26*
The Lord spoke to him while a youth   *1 Sam. 3:11*
Judge of Israel   *1 Sam. 7:3–8:22*
Anointed Saul king   *1 Sam. 10:1*
Rebuked Saul for sin   *1 Sam. 13:13*
Anointed David king   *1 Sam. 16:1–13*
His faith commended   *Ps. 99:6; Acts 3:24; Heb. 11:32*

Sanctification (See also Consecration, Holiness, Justification)
Of believers in Christ   *1 Cor. 1:2; 6:11; Heb. 10:10, 14*
By Christ's power   *Phil. 3:21*
Through faith   *Acts 26:18*

Through the Spirit   *1 Pet. 1:2*
Willed by God   *1 Thess. 4:3*

Sanctuary (See also Holy Place, Tabernacle)
Lord's dwelling place   *Gen. 28:16; Ps. 11:4*
Beauty of   *Ps. 96:6*
Holiness of   *1 Cor. 3:17*
To be revered   *Lev. 19:30; John 2:16*

Sanhedrin (See also Pharisees, Sadducees)
Jesus' appearance before   *Luke 22:66; John 18:19*
Apostles' appearance before   *Acts 6:27*
Gamaliel, a member of   *Acts 5:34*

Sanitation (See also Cleanliness, Purity)
■ Commands regarding:
    Washing   *Deut. 23:10–11*
    Burning   *Num. 31:19–23*
    Covering filth   *Deut. 23:12*
    Dead bodies   *Lev. 11:24–40*
    Leprosy   *Lev. 13:2–59*
    Human discharge   *Lev. 15:1–30*

Sapphira (See Ananias)

Sarah (See also Abraham)
Wife of Abraham   *Gen. 11:29*
Called Abraham's sister   *Gen. 12:10–20*
Gave birth to a son in her old age   *Gen. 21:2*

Satan (See also Demon, Devil, Evil)
As the serpent   *Gen. 3:4*
Responsible for Job's suffering   *Job 1:6–12; 2:1–7*
Temptation of Jesus by   *Matt. 4:1–11*
God of this world   *2 Cor. 4:4*
Adversary of believers   *1 Pet. 5:8*
Power of contrasted with God's power   *Acts 26:18*
To be tormented forever   *Rev. 20:10*

Saul, King
Anointing of   *1 Sam. 11:6*
Tried to kill David   *1 Sam. 19:1–10*
Committed suicide   *1 Sam. 31:4*

Saul of Tarsus (See Paul)

Savior (See also Jesus Christ)
Identified as God   *Ps. 106:21*
Applied to Christ   *2 Tim. 1:10*
Believed to be   *John 4:42*
■ Described by:
   Prophets   *Isa. 42:6–7*
   Angels   *Matt. 1:20–21*
   John the Baptist   *John 1:29*
   Peter   *Acts 5:31*
   Paul   *1 Tim. 1:15*
   John   *1 John 4:14*

Scapegoat (See also Sacrifice)
Presented alive   *Lev. 16:10, 20–22*

Scepter (See also Ruler)
Symbol of authority from Israel   *Num. 24:17*
Extended by King   *Esther 5:2*
Symbol of righteousness   *Heb. 1:8*

School (See also Teacher)
In home   *Deut. 6:6–9*
Music training for temple   *1 Chron. 25:1–8*

Scoff, Scoffers (See also Mocking)
Appearing in the last days   *2 Pet. 3:3*
Blind man abused by   *John 9:28*
At Pentecost   *Acts 2:13*
Questions by   *Ps. 42:10; 73:11; 78:19*

Scribe (See also Law, Pharisees, Writing)
Instructor of Law   *Matt. 7:29*
Lacked righteousness   *Matt. 5:20*
Jesus warned   *Mark 12:38–40*
Wisdom of, was foolish   *1 Cor. 1:20*
Jesus suffered at hands of   *Matt. 16:21*

Scripture (See also Inspiration, Revelation, Word of God)
Given by God   *2 Tim. 3:16*
Inspired by Holy Spirit   *Acts 1:16; 2 Pet. 1:21*
Christ taught   *Luke 24:27*
For instruction   *Rom. 15:4*
Bears witness to Christ   *John 5:39–40*
To cleanse   *Eph. 5:26*
Called Sword of the Spirit   *Eph. 6:17*
Likened to a lamp   *2 Pet. 1:19*
Presents way of salvation   *2 Tim. 3:15*

Sea (See also Red Sea)
Pharaoh and his army destroyed in   *Exod. 15:4*
Jesus walking beside   *Matt. 4:18*
Gives up dead at judgment   *Rev. 20:13*

Seal
Of righteousness   *Rom. 4:11*
Of apostleship   *1 Cor. 9:2*
Of Holy Spirit   *2 Cor. 1:22*
Christ worthy to open   *Rev. 5:9*

Season
Origin of   *Gen. 1:14*
Change of will continue   *Gen. 8:22*
For everything   *Eccles. 3:1*

Second Coming (See also Antichrist)
Signs of   *Matt. 24:4–25*

Events of   *Matt. 24:26–44; Luke 21:25–28*
Described   *1 Thess. 4:13–18*
Foretold   *Acts 1:9–11*
Promise of   *John 14:3*

Second Death (See also Hell)
To everlasting contempt   *Dan. 12:2*
To the lake of fire   *Rev. 20:14*
A resurrection of judgment   *John 5:29*
To escape from   *John 8:51; Rev. 2:11*

Secret (See also Mystery)
Belongs to the Lord   *Deut. 29:29*
Of men to be judged   *Eccles. 12:14; Rom. 2:16*
Sins known by God   *Ps. 90:8*
Deeds exposed   *John 3:20*
Of the heart revealed   *1 Cor. 14:25*

Security (See also Peace, Protection)
With Christ   *Heb. 6:19*
Of a heavenly body   *2 Cor. 5:1–5*
In the New Earth   *Isa. 11:6*

Self-acceptance (See also Self-examination)
■ Of believers:
In knowing forgiveness of sins   *Col. 1:14*
In knowing God's acceptance of them   *Eph. 2:19–22*
In recognizing gift   *1 Cor. 12:4–6, 12–31*

Self-control (See also Character)
A Christian virtue   *2 Pet. 1:6*
■ Elements of:
Control of one's body   *1 Cor. 9:27*
Sober judgment   *Rom. 12:3*
Control of one's temper   *Prov. 16:32*
Of Jesus   *Matt. 27:12–14*
Urged in light of Christ's return   *1 Thess. 5:6*

Self-defense
Jesus', in his trial   *Mark 15:2-5; Luke 23:3*
Protected under Jewish law   *John 7:51*

Self-delusion (See also Pride)
- Contributing factors:
  Natural wisdom   *Prov. 14:12*
  False teaching   *1 Thess. 5:3*
  False view of God   *2 Pet. 3:3-5*

Self-denial (See also Humility, Self-control)
- Described as:
  Denial   *Titus 2:12; 1 Pet. 4:2*
  Putting to death   *Col. 3:5*
  Renunciation   *Luke 14:33*
  Putting off   *Eph. 4:22*
  Taking up the cross   *Matt. 10:38*
- Commended as:
  Spiritual worship   *Rom. 12:1-2*
  Expression of love   *Rom. 16:4*
  Worthy of reward   *Luke 18:28-30*

Self-examination (See also Self-acceptance)
- By means of:
  God's Word   *Ps. 119:59; Heb. 4:12*
  Christ's example   *Heb. 12:1-2*
  God himself   *Job 13:23; Ps. 26:2; 139:23*
- Purposes of:
  Preparation for Lord's Supper   *1 Cor. 11:28-32*
  Test of one's faith   *2 Cor. 13:5*
  Test of one's works   *Gal. 6:4*

Self-indulgence (See also Self-control)
- Instances of:
  Solomon   *Eccles. 2:10; 8:15*
  The rich fool   *Luke 12:16-20*
Judged   *Eccles. 11:9*

Selfishness (See also Behavior, Self-indulgence, Submission)
- Exemplified in:
  Self-love   *2 Tim. 3:2*
  Self-seeking   *Phil. 2:21*
- Avoided by:
  Service to others   *Rom. 15:2-3; 1 Cor. 10:24*
  Following Christ's example   *Mark 10:43-45*
  Submission to Christ   *Phil. 1:21*
  Manifesting love   *1 Cor. 3:5*

Self-righteousness (See also Humility, Righteousness)
- Described as:
  Presumptuous   *Deut. 9:4-6*
  Unprofitable   *Isa. 57:12*
  Offensive   *Isa. 64:6; 65:4*
  Outward show   *Matt. 23:25-28*
  Rejecting God's righteousness   *Rom. 10:3*

Self-will (See also Self-control)
- Revealed in:
  Presumption   *Num. 14:40-45; Neh. 9:16-17*
  Rebellious attitude towards parents   *Deut. 21:18-21*
  Stubbornness   *Isa. 48:4-8*

Sensuality (See also Idolatry, Immorality, Pleasure)
Manifested in divisive, ungodly men   *Jude 18-19*
Associated with worldly wisdom   *James 3:15*
Encouraged if no resurrection   *1 Cor. 15:32*

Seraphim (See also Angels, Cherubim)
Description   *Isa. 6:2-7*

Sermon (See also Preaching, Teaching)
On the Mount   *Matt. 5:7*

Of Peter   *Acts 2:14–36; 3:12–26*
Of Stephen   *Acts 7:2–53*
Of Paul in Athens   *Acts 17:18, 22–31*

Serpent (See also Devil)

In temptation of man   *Gen. 3:1–19; 2 Cor. 11:3*
Cursed   *Gen. 3:14*
■ Miracles associated with:
   Moses' rod   *Exod. 4:3; 7:9–10*
   Hebrews cured by   *Num. 21:8–9*

Servant (See also Bondage, Ministry)

■ Christ is:
   Of man   *Matt. 20:28; Luke 22:27*
   Bond-servant   *Phil. 2:7–8*
■ Of Christ:
   To be content   *1 Cor. 7:20–21*
   Paul   *Phil. 1:1; Titus 1:1*
■ Duties:
   Honor master   *Mal. 1:6; 1 Tim. 6:1*
   Obey master   *Eph. 6:5; Titus 2:9*

Seth

Third son of Adam   *Gen. 4:25; 5:3*

Seven

Days for Feast of Tabernacles   *Exod. 12:15–19*
Day of the week to rest   *Exod. 20:10*
The sabbatical year   *Lev. 25:2–6*
Times around Jericho   *Josh. 6:4*

Seventy

Elders to assist Moses   *Num. 11:16*
Years in Babylonian exile   *Jer. 25:11*
Weeks of redemption   *Dan. 9:24*
Times seven   *Matt. 18:22*
Jesus sends   *Luke 10:1*

Sexual Conduct (See also Celibacy, Lust, Marriage)

As intercourse   *Gen. 4:1*
As union   *Gen. 2:24; Exod. 22:16; 1 Cor. 6:16*
As privilege of marriage   *1 Cor. 7:3-5*
Unrighteous out of marriage   *1 Cor. 6:9-10*

Shadrach (See also Abednego)

Deliverance from furnace   *Dan. 1:1-7; 3:1-30*

Shame (See also Guilt, Remorse)

Of Adam and Eve   *Gen. 3:7-10*
Of those who disregard God's law   *Hos. 4:6-7*
Of those who deny Jesus   *Mark 8:38; Luke 9:26*
Suffered for Christ's sake   *Acts 5:41*
Is glory of enemies of cross   *Phil. 3:19*
Of the cross   *Heb. 12:2*
Avoid by abiding in Christ   *1 John 2:28*

Sheba, Queen of

Visited Solomon   *1 Kings 10:1-13*

Sheep (See also Animal, Sacrifice)

- Literal:
    As sacrifice   *Gen. 4:4; 8:20; 22:13*
    Jacob cares for   *Gen. 30:32-40*
- Figurative:
    As servants of God   *Ps. 100:3; John 21:15-17*
    Of mankind   *Isa. 53:6*
    Of innocence   *Matt. 7:15*
    Of sinner in parable   *Matt. 18:11-13; Luke 15:4-7*

Shem

Son of Noah   *Gen. 5:32; 9:26; 1 Chron. 1:17-27*

Sheol (See also Death)

God's anger burns there   *Deut. 32:22*

A place of abandonment   *Ps. 16:10*
A place of the dead   *Ezek. 32:21*

Shepherd (See also Parable, Pastor)
■ Duties:
   To provide food   *Ps. 23:2*
   To watch strays   *Matt. 18:12*
   To protect   *1 Sam. 17:34–35; Amos 3:12*
■ Figurative of:
   God's provision   *Ps. 23; 78:52; 80:1*
   Prophets and priests   *Ezek. 34*
   Jesus   *John 10:11; 1 Pet. 2:25*

Shewbread, Showbread (See also Tabernacle)
In tabernacle   *Exod 25:30; Lev. 24:8*
Description of   *Lev. 24:5–6*
As an offering   *Lev. 24:7*
Food for High Priest's family   *Lev. 24:9*
David asked for   *1 Sam. 21:1–6*

Shield (See also Armor)
■ Made of:
   Gold   *2 Sam. 8:7; 1 Kings 10:16*
   Bronze   *1 Kings 14:27*
■ Figurative of:
   God   *Gen. 15:1; Deut. 33:29; 2 Sam. 22:3*
   God's faithfulness   *Ps. 91:4*
   Faith   *Eph. 6:16*
   Salvation   *2 Sam. 22:36*

Shiloh
Site of tabernacle   *Josh. 18:1; Judg. 21:19*

Shimei
Cursed David   *2 Sam. 16:5*
Killed by Solomon   *1 Kings 2:36*

Sickness (See also Health, Disease, Medicine)
Under God's control   *Deut. 32:39; 1 Cor. 11:30*
Because of sin   *Lev. 26:14-16; 2 Chron. 21:12-15*
Result of excesses   *Hos. 7:5; Prov. 25:16*
Christ healed   *Matt. 4:23; 8:3, 13; Mark 10:52*
Pray for those in   *Acts 28:8; James 5:14-15*

Sign (See also Miracle)
■ A distinctive mark:
  Of God's work   *Exod. 4:28-30; 7:3-5; Acts 2:43*
  Of a prophecy   *1 Sam. 10:1-8; Isa. 7:11-14*
  Of God's messenger   *Matt. 12:38-40; John 2:11*
  Of end times   *Luke 21:11, 25*

Silas
Leader in Jerusalem sent with Paul   *Acts 15:22*
Imprisoned with Paul at Philippi   *Acts 16:16-40*

Silver (See also Gold, Money)
As money   *Gen. 17:12; Matt. 10:9*
In tabernacle   *Exod. 26:19; Num. 7:13*
In temple   *1 Chron. 28:14; 29:2-5; Ezra 5:14*

Simeon
Son of Jacob   *Gen. 29:33*
His descendants   *Gen. 46:10; Exod. 6:15*
Prophesied concerning infant Jesus   *Luke 2:25-35*

Simon (See Peter)

Sin (See also Guilt, Sinner, Wickedness)
Known of God   *Gen. 3:11; Ps. 44:21; 69:5; Matt. 10:26*
God's displeasure in   *Gen. 6:6; Deut. 25:16; Ps. 5:4*
Righteous do not condone   *Gen. 39:9; Deut. 7:26*
Consequences of   *Exod. 20:5; Prov. 14:11; Rom. 5:12*
Forgiveness of   *Exod. 34:7; Matt. 26:28*
Confession of   *Neh. 1:6; James 5:16; 1 John 1:9*

Jesus takes away   *John 1:29; 2 Cor. 5:21*

Sinai, Mount
Where Commandments were given   *Gen. 19:1–25*

Sincerity (See also Honesty, Integrity)
Of forgiveness   *Matt. 18:21–22*
Of faith   *1 Tim. 1:5*
Of ministers   *Titus 2:7*
Of Jesus   *1 Pet. 2:22*
■ Of Christian love:
For others   *Rom. 12:9; 1 Pet. 1:22; 1 John 3:18*
For God   *Deut. 6:5*
For Christ   *Eph. 6:24*

Singing (See also Music, Voice)
■ Because of rejoicing:
For friend   *Gen. 31:27*
For victory   *Exod. 15:1*
At feasts   *Isa. 5:12; Amos 6:5*
In prison   *Acts 16:25*

Sinlessness (See also Perfection)
Of Christ   *Luke 1:35; John 8:46; 2 Cor. 5:21*
Beyond human ability   *Rom. 3:23; 1 John 1:8*

Sinner (See also Evil, Sin, Unbeliever)
Class of all men   *Rom. 3:23*
Punishment of   *Prov. 11:31; Rom. 6:23*
■ Jesus' relationship to:
Friend of   *Luke 7:34*
Came to invite   *Luke 5:32*
Welcomes   *Luke 15:1–2*
Savior   *Acts 2:36–38*

Slander (See also Backbiting, Gossip, Tongue)
Do not listen to   *1 Sam. 24:9*
Bad effects of   *Prov. 16:28; 18:8; 19:9; 26:20*

Enduring for Christ's sake   *Matt. 5:11*
Of evil heart   *Luke 6:45*
Returning good for   *1 Cor. 4:13*
Christians should not   *2 Cor. 12:20; Eph. 4:29–31*

Sleep (See also Insomnia, Rest)

Supernaturally caused   *Gen. 2:21; 1 Sam. 26:12*
Visions in   *Gen. 28:10; 1 Sam. 3:2–18; Dan. 8:18*
Meaning physical death   *John 11:11–14*
Of the lazy   *Prov. 6:9–10; 24:33*
Of disciples   *Matt. 26:40–43*
Figuratively, spiritual state of the unsaved   *Eph. 5:14*

Smoking (See Health)

Social Reform (See also Justice, Poverty, Society)

How to help the poor   *Prov. 19:17; 22:2, 9; Luke 3:11*
How to treat the poor   *Prov. 14:20–21, 31; 19:7*

Society (See also Justice, Liberality, Witnessing)

■ Christian's responsibility:
  To be salt   *Matt. 5:13*
  To be light   *Matt. 5:14; Gal. 6:10*
  To obey those in authority   *Rom. 13:1*
  To pay taxes   *Rom. 13:6–7*
  To witness   *1 Pet. 2:9–10*
  To act justly and love mercy   *Isa. 1:16–17; Mic. 6:8*

Sodom (See also Gomorrah)

Its sin and destruction   *Gen. 13:13; 18:20–19:29*
Lot escaped   *Gen. 19:1–26*
An example of God's judgment   *Matt. 10:15;
  Luke 17:29; Rev. 11:8*

Soldier (See also Battle, War)

Of Israel   *Num. 1:2*
Mocked Jesus   *Matt. 27:27–31*

Crucified Jesus   *Matt. 27:27, 31–37; John 19:23–24*
Guarding tomb   *Matt. 27:65; 28:4, 11–15*

Solomon
Birth and parents of   *2 Sam. 5:14*
Rise to kingship   *1 Kings 1:28*
Wisdom of   *1 Kings 4:29–31*
Folly of   *1 Kings 11:1–8*
Built temple   *1 Kings 6:1*

Son (See also Adoption, Daughter, Family)
Of Man   *Matt. 12:40; 24:37–44; Luke 19:10*
Of God—Christ   *Mark 1:1; Luke 1:35; John 1:34*
Of God—believer   *Gal. 3:26*

Song (See also Hymn, Music, Singing)
Of praise   *2 Chron. 5:13; Acts 16:25*
New   *Ps. 33:3*
At Passover   *Matt. 26:30*
Spiritual   *Eph. 5:19; Col. 3:16*

Sorrow (See also Grief, Mourning, Tear)
God sees   *Gen. 21:17–20; Exod. 3:7–10*
Of Jacob for Joseph   *Gen. 37:34–35*
Shall go away   *Isa. 35:10*
Of Jesus   *Isa. 53:11; Matt. 26:37–44*
Of the lost   *Matt. 8:12; 13:42, 50; 22:13*
Because of sin   *2 Cor. 7:10–11*
None in heaven   *Rev. 21:4*

Soul (See also Heart, Mind, Person)
Man became a living   *Gen. 2:7*
At death   *Gen. 35:18*
Loving God with all of   *Matt. 22:37*
To serve with   *Josh. 22:5*
Impatience of   *Num. 21:4*
Redemption of   *Lev. 17:11*
Worth of   *Matt. 16:26*

Sovereignty (See also Authority, Ruler)
- Of God:
  His ownership   *Ps. 24:1; 50:10*
  His reign   *Exod. 15:18; Josh. 2:11; Rom. 14:11*
  His greatness   *Exod. 18:11; Deut. 4:39; 10:14*
  Over life   *1 Sam. 2:6; Dan. 5:23; Col. 1:17*
  Over man's ways   *1 Sam. 2:7-8; Job 34:24;
     John 19:11*
  Over salvation   *John 10:29; James 4:12*

Speech (See also Conversation, Tongue, Voice)
With grace   *Col. 4:6*
Moses claimed to be slow of .   *Exod. 4:10*
Paul's was not eloquent   *1 Cor. 1:17*
Of false teachers   *Rom. 16:18*

Spirit (See also Fruit of the Spirit, Holy Spirit)
Of evil   *1 Sam. 16:16; 18:10; Hos. 4:12*
Holy   *Ps. 51:11; Isa. 63:10; Matt. 12:32*
Control of one's   *Prov. 16:32; 25:28*
Body apart from   *James 2:26*
Does not die with body   *Matt. 27:50; Acts 7:59*

Spiritualism (See also Occult, Spirit, Witchcraft)
Condemned   *Lev. 19:26; Deut. 18:9-14; Isa. 47:13*
Of mediums   *Deut. 18:11; 1 Sam. 28:8; 2 Kings 21:6*
As divination   *1 Sam. 15:23; Ezek. 21:21*

Spirituality (See also Discipleship, Holy Spirit,
   Sanctification)
- True:
  Because of Holy Spirit   *Rom. 8:4*
  Devotion to God   *Deut. 6:5; 1 Kings 8:23*
  Trust   *Isa. 26:3; Rom. 8:6*
  Perception   *Mark 2:8; Acts 17:16; Gal. 6:1*
  Discernment   *John 16:13; 1 Cor. 2:14-15*
  Holiness   *2 Cor. 7:1; Col. 2:5*

Spring (See also Thirst, Water)
Source of water for earth   *Ps. 104:10*
Jesus asked for drink from   *John 4:7*
Cannot produce two kinds of water   *James 3:11*
Without water likened to deceiver   *2 Pet. 2:17*
Which gives eternal life   *John 4:13–14*

Sprinkling (See also Sacrifice)
■ Of blood:
  For tabernacle and people   *Lev. 8:15, 19*
  For leper   *Lev. 14:7*
  To cleanse flesh   *Heb. 9:13*
  Of Christ, figuratively   *1 Pet. 1:2*
■ Of water:
  For Levites   *Num. 8:7*
  For Israel   *Ezek. 36:25*
  For tabernacle and people   *Heb. 9:19–22*

Star (See also Astrology, Astronomy, Sun)
Created by God   *Gen. 1:16; Ps. 8:3*
Worshiped   *Jer. 8:2*
Of Bethlehem   *Matt. 2:2*

State (See also Government, Nation, Society)
God over Israel   *Exod. 19:5–6*
Has its own rights   *Luke 20:25*
Exists by God's grace   *John 19:11*
Christians are to support   *Rom. 13:1–7; 1 Tim. 2:2*

Steadfastness (See also Faithfulness, Long-suffering, Patience)
Of God   *Num. 23:19; James 1:17*
In affliction   *Ps. 44:17–19; 1 Thess. 3:3*
In the early church   *Acts 2:42*
In the faith   *1 Cor. 16:13*
Commanded   *Phil. 4:1; 2 Thess. 2:15; James 1:6–8*
In confidence   *Heb. 3:6, 14*

Stealing (See Deceit, Dishonesty, Robbery)
Condemned   *Exod. 20:15; Deut. 5:19; Matt. 19:18*
Repayment for   *Exod. 22:1–15; Lev. 6:4–5*
Causes shame   *Jer. 2:26*
Work instead of   *Eph. 4:28*

Stephen (See also Martyrdom)
Chosen as deacon   *Acts 6:5*
Arrested   *Acts 6:8–15*
His sermon   *Acts 7:1–53*
Was stoned to death   *Acts 7:54–60*

Sterility (See also Barrenness)
Viewed as a reproach   *Gen. 30:22–23*
Healed by God   *Gen. 17:15–21; 25:21; 1 Sam. 1:6–20*

Stone (See also Foundation)
■ Figurative:
   Of offense   *Isa. 8:14; Rom. 9:33; 1 Pet. 2:8*
   Of hard heart   *Ezek. 36:26*
   Of Christ   *Matt. 21:42; Acts 4:11; 1 Pet. 2:4*

Stoning
As capital punishment   *Exod. 19:13; Heb. 11:37*
Of Sabbath breaker   *Num. 15:36*
Required witnesses   *Deut. 13:9*
Of Achan   *Josh. 7:25*
Of Naboth   *1 Kings 21:13*
Of Stephen   *Acts 7:59*
Of Paul   *Acts 14:19; 2 Cor. 11:25*

Strength (See also Power, Weakness)
Of the Lord   *Exod. 13:3, 14, 16*
Of man   *Exod. 15:2; Ps. 28:7; 46:1*
Given to the weak by God   *Isa. 40:29*
Loving God with   *Mark 12:30*
Supplied by God   *1 Pet. 4:11*

Stress (See also Anxiety, Care, Worry)
Exhibited by Paul   1 Cor. 2:3; 2 Cor. 7:5
Eased by Titus and the Corinthians   2 Cor. 7:6–7
Exhibited by Christ   Luke 22:42–44

Strife (See also Arguing, Quarrel)
Avoided   Prov. 15:18
Spread by the perverse   Prov. 16:28
Is difficult to stop   Prov. 17:14
Brought by fools   Prov. 18:6
Not to be among Christians   Rom. 13:13; 1 Cor. 3:3
Leads to confusion and evil   James 3:16

Stubbornness (See also Pride, Rebellion)
Of Pharaoh   Exod. 4:21; 7:3, 13, 22
In believing   2 Chron. 36:15–16
In not listening   Prov. 1:24
In resisting the Holy Spirit   Acts 7:51
In not repenting   Rom. 2:5

Stumbling (See also Stone)
Caused by sin   Ezek. 7:19; Rom. 11:9–11
■ Block (stone):
  The blind   Lev. 19:14
■ Figurative:
  As an offense   Rom. 9:32–33
  Not causing a brother's   Rom. 14:13; 1 Cor. 8:9

Submission (See also Humility, Love, Servant)
To righteousness of God   Rom. 10:3
To one another   Eph. 5:21
Of wife to husband   Eph. 5:22; Col. 3:18
To human institution   1 Pet. 2:13
To elders   1 Pet. 5:5
To leaders   Heb. 13:7
To God   James 4:7

Substitution (See also Atonement)

Of offering for offerer   *Lev. 1:4; 16:21–22*
Of Jesus for Barabbas   *Matt. 27:20; Mark 15:11*
Dying in place of a friend   *John 15:13*
Christ's suffering in place of man's   *1 Pet. 2:21*

Success (See also Blessing, Reward)

- Obtained by:
  Requesting from God   *Gen. 24:12*
  Keeping God's Word   *Josh. 1:8*
- As prosperity:
  From God   *Gen. 33:11; Ps. 127:1; 128:1–2*
  Danger of   *Deut. 8:10–18; 2 Chron. 12:1; 26:16*

Suffering (See also Adversity, Affliction, Pain)

Because of sin   *Gen. 3:15–19; Hos. 8:7; Gal. 6:8*
As a chastisement   *Judg. 2:22–3:6; Prov. 3:12*
As a test   *Ps. 66:10; James 1:3, 12; 1 Pet. 1:7*
God's presence in   *Ps. 73:21–26*
In God's control   *Isa. 45:7; Amos 3:6; Acts 2:23*
Sharing in Christ's   *Mark 10:39; Rom. 8:17*
Of Christ   *Heb. 12:2; 1 Pet. 1:10–12; 2:24*

Suicide

Of Saul   *1 Sam. 31:4*
Of Saul's armor bearer   *1 Sam. 31:5*
Of Judas   *Matt. 27:5*
Saving jailer from   *Acts 16:27–28*
Jews question Jesus' intent   *John 8:22*

Sun

Made by God   *Gen. 1:16*
Stood still   *Josh. 10:13*
Protection from   *Ps. 121:6*
- Figuratively:
  Of the righteous   *Matt. 13:43*
  Of Christ's glory   *Matt. 17:2*

Sunday (See Lord's Day)

Superstition (See also Idolatry)
- Instances of:
  Burning incense to restore prosperity
    Jer. 44:17-19
  Bringing the ark to assure victory   *1 Sam. 4:3-10*
  Casting lots to determine who caused evil
    Jon 1:7-8
  Jews used in accusing Paul   *Acts 25:19*

Supper (See also Last Supper)
Christ and disciples   *Matt. 26:17-30*
Communion   *1 Cor. 11:20-32*
For believers in heaven   *Rev. 19:9*
For those who can't reciprocate   *Luke 14:12-14*
In honor of Jesus   *John 12:2*

Swearing (See also Blasphemy, Oath)
To not deal falsely   *Gen. 21:23-24*
By the name of the Lord   *Isa. 48:1*
As cursing   *Mark 14:71*
Jesus preached against   *Matt. 5:34-37*
By God in his covenant with Abraham   *Heb. 6:13*

Sword (See also Armor, Judgment, War)
Flaming   *Gen. 3:24*
Beat into plowshares   *Mic. 4:3*
Christ warns about use of   *Matt. 26:51-52*
James killed by   *Acts 12:2*
- Figuratively:
  Two-edged   *Rev. 1:16*
  Of the Word of God   *Heb. 4:12*
  Of the Spirit   *Eph. 6:17*

Symbol (See also Cross, Communion, Type)
Rainbow   *Gen. 9:13-15*

Oil   *Ps. 45:7*
Water   *Eph. 5:26*
Dove   *Matt. 3:16*
Smitten rock   *1 Cor. 10:4*
Baptism   *Rom. 6:3–4*
Lord's Supper   *1 Cor. 11:23–26*

Sympathy (See also Compassion, Pity)

For prisoners   *Heb. 13:3*
For fatherless and widows   *James 1:27*
For one another   *1 Pet. 3:8*
For the multitudes   *Matt. 15:32*
Of God   *Jon. 4:2*
Such as Christ showed   *Phil. 2:2–5*

Synagogue (See also Church, Temple)

Hypocritical giving in   *Matt. 6:2*
Pharisees love chief seats in   *Matt. 23:6*
Christ read and interpreted Scripture in   *Luke 4:16–27*
Persecuted in   *Mark 13:9*

T

Tabernacle (See also Ark of the Covenant)
Instruction for building   *Exod. 26*
Completed   *Exod. 39:32*
Glory of the Lord filled   *Exod. 40:34*
True one set up by the Lord   *Heb. 8:2*
■ Figuratively:
   Of the body   *2 Pet. 1:13–14*
   Of God's presence with man   *Rev. 21:3*

Table (See also Lord's Supper)
For the shewbread   *Exod. 25:30*
Of the Lord   *1 Cor. 10:21*
Christ betrayed at   *Luke 22:21*
To serve, indicating charitable work   *Acts 6:2*
Of stone   *Exod. 24:12*

Tact (See Discretion, Mouth, Prudence)

Talent (See also Creativity, Gift)
Not to neglect   *1 Tim. 4:14*
Parable on use of   *Matt. 25:14–30*
Use of according to ability   *Rom. 12:6*
To use for one another   *1 Pet. 4:10*

Tarshish
Where Jonah headed in disobedience   *Jon. 1:3*
Prophecies concerning   *Ps. 48:7; 72:10; Isa. 2:16; 60:9*

Tarsus
Apostle Paul's hometown   *Acts 9:11*

Taxes (See also Publican)
Collectors of   *Matt. 5:46*
Of Caesar Augustus   *Luke 2:1*
Jesus paid   *Matt. 17:24*

Jesus ate with collectors of   *Mark 2:16*
Commanded to pay   *Rom. 13:6–7*
To Caesar   *Matt. 22:17–21*

Teacher (See also Instruction, Learning, Wisdom)
In early church   *Acts 13:1*
Gift to the church   *Eph. 4:11*
Warning against false   *2 Pet. 2:1*
Christ as   *Mark 1:21–22; Luke 24:27; John 7:14*
Holy Spirit as   *John 14:26*

Teaching (See also Doctrine, Law)
Of Christ   *Matt. 5:1–12*
For meditation   *Ps. 119:15–16*
Christ questioned about his   *John 18:19*
Scripture profitable for   *2 Tim. 3:16*
People astonished at   *Matt. 7:28*
Disciples how to pray   *Luke 11:1*

Tear (See also Sorrow, Weeping)
Poured out to God   *Job 16:20*
Washed Christ's feet with   *Luke 7:38*
Of Christ   *Heb. 5:7*
God shall wipe away   *Rev. 7:17*
Absence of in heaven   *Rev. 21:4*

Temperance (See Abstinence from alcohol, Drunkenness, Liberty)

Temple (See also Synagogue)
House of the Lord   *1 Kings 6:1–2*
God's glory in   *Isa. 6:1*
Herod's   *John 2:20*
Early Christians met in   *Acts 2:46*
Jesus drove money makers out of   *Luke 19:45*
■ Figurative:
  Of Christ's body   *John 2:19–22*
  Of Christian's body   *1 Cor. 3:16–17*

Temptation (See also Trial)
By Satan in garden   *Gen. 3:1–5*
Eve yielded to   *Gen. 3:6*
Prayer to avoid   *Matt. 6:13*
Of Christ by Satan   *Luke 4:1–13*
Common to all   *1 Cor. 10:13*
Reward for enduring   *James 1:12*
Is not from God   *James 1:13–14*

Ten Commandments (See also Commandment, Law, Moses)
Given by God   *Exod. 20:1–17*
Referred to by Christ   *Matt. 5:21, 27, 31, 33, 38, 43*
Bring knowledge of sin   *Rom. 7:7*
Summed up   *Rom. 13:9*

Tenderness (See also Gentleness, Kindness)
Shown to one another   *Eph. 4:32*
Of Christ in Paul's life   *2 Cor. 10:1*
Characteristic of God   *James 5:11*

Tent (See also Tabernacle)
Of meeting   *Num. 2:17*
Ark of Covenant in   *1 Chron. 16:1*
Made by Paul, Priscilla, and Aquila   *Acts 18:2–3*
■ Figurative:
   Of the heavens   *Isa. 40:22*
   Of growth of Israel   *Isa. 54:2*

Testament (See also Covenant, Promise)
Symbols of the New   *Matt. 26:28; Luke 22:20*
Ministers of the New   *2 Cor. 3:6*
Reading of the Old   *2 Cor. 3:14*
Christ mediator of a New   *Heb. 9:15*

Testimony (See also Covenant, Law, Witnessing)
Placed in the ark   *Exod. 25:16*

Of God's majesty to others   *Ps. 145:11–12*
Of the Lord   *Ps. 19:7*
Believed by others   *2 Thess. 1:10*
Not to be ashamed of giving   *2 Tim. 1:8*

Thaddeus (See also Judas)
Chosen as apostle   *Matt. 10:3*

Thankfulness (See also Gratitude, Ingratitude, Thanksgiving)
God's will for believers   *Col. 4:12; 1 Thess. 5:18*
In Christ's name   *Eph. 5:20*
■ Expressed for:
  Wisdom   *Dan. 2:23*
  Answered prayer   *John 11:41*
  Salvation   *2 Cor. 9:15*
  Food   *John 6:11, 23*

Thanksgiving (See also Praise, Thankfulness, Worship)
Offered to God   *Ps. 69:30; 100:4; 147:7*
To accompany prayer   *Phil. 4:6*
Response of believer   *Col. 2:7*

Theophilus
To whom Luke's gospel is addressed   *Luke 1:3*

Thessalonica
Paul's journey there   *Acts 17:1*

Thief (See also Robbery, Stealing)
Crucified with Christ   *Matt. 27:38, 44; Mark 15:27*
The Day of the Lord will come as a   *1 Thess. 5:2*
Behavior condemned   *Exod. 20:15*

Thirst (See also Water)
■ Figurative of:
  Salvation   *Isa. 55:1; John 7:37; Eph. 4:28*

   Desire to know God   *Ps. 42:1; 63:1*
   Longing for righteousness   *Matt. 5:6*
Satisfied   *Rev. 7:16*

Thomas (See also Apostle)
Disciple of Jesus   *Matt. 10:3*
Willing to die with Jesus   *John 11:16*
Resurrection appearances to   *John 20:19–29*
Present in upper room   *Acts 1:13*

Throne (See also King)
Men's, established through righteousness   *Prov. 16:12*
David's promised to Jesus Christ   *Luke 1:30–32*
Christ's eternal   *Luke 1:32–33*
Christ now rules from   *Eph. 1:20–23; Heb. 1:3*
Christ will judge from   *Matt. 25:31–32*

Time (See also Season)
Right, to respond to the gospel   *Mark 1:15*
Should be used carefully   *Eph. 5:16*
Christ born at the right   *Gal. 4:4*
Of Christ's return unknown   *Matt. 24:36*
Appropriate, for different events   *Eccles. 3:1–8*

Timothy
Faith from childhood   *2 Tim. 1:5*
Became Paul's assistant   *Acts 16:1–3*
Ordained by elders   *1 Tim. 4:14*
Loyal worker   *Phil. 2:22*
Loved by Paul   *1 Tim. 1:18*
Imitator of Paul   *1 Cor. 4:17*
Prone to sickness   *1 Tim. 5:23*

Tithe (See also Offering)
Given by Abraham to Melchizedek   *Heb. 7:1–2, 6*
Possession of the Lord   *Lev. 27:30–33*
Provision for Levites   *Num. 18:21–24*
Promise regarding   *Mal. 3:10–12*

Legalistic practice of Pharisees condemned   *Luke 11:42; 18:9–14*

Titus
Greek coworker with Paul   *Gal. 2:3; 2 Cor. 7:6*
Paul's letter to   *Titus 1:1*

Tolerance (See also Intolerance, Patience)
Religious   *Luke 9:49–50*
With a weaker brother   *Rom. 14:1–18*
Inappropriate when treating sin   *Mark 9:43–48*

Tongue (See also Conversation, Mouth, Speech)
Powerful instrument for good or evil   *James 3:5–11*
To be guarded carefully   *Ps. 39:1; Prov. 21:23*
∎ Proper use of:
  To proclaim God's righteousness   *Ps. 35:28*
  To speak on behalf of justice   *Ps. 37:30*
  To sing   *Ps. 119:172; 126:2*
  To confess Christ   *Phil. 2:11*

Tongues, Gift of (See also Baptism)
Experienced at Pentecost   *Acts 2:1–11*
Gift of the Holy Spirit   *1 Cor. 12:10–11*
Interpreter required   *1 Cor. 14:27–28*

Torment (See also Suffering)
Eternal   *Rev. 14:9–11, 20:10*
Physical   *Matt. 8:6*
Experienced by faithful   *Heb. 11:35–39*

Tradition (See also Law, Teaching)
Reject worldly   *Col. 2:8*
∎ Christian, described:
  Fundamental truths   *1 Cor. 15:3*
  Passed on by apostles   *2 Thess. 3:6–7; 2 Thess. 2:15*
  Based on eyewitness reports   *2 Pet. 1:16*
  Originating with Christ   *1 Cor. 11:1, 23–26*

Treachery (See also Deceit, Dishonesty)
- Revealed in:
  Judas   *Matt. 26:47–50; Mark 14:43–46*
  David   *2 Sam. 11:14–15*
  Absalom   *2 Sam. 13:23–29*
  Haman   *Esther 3:5–11*

Treason (See also Patriotism)
- Examples of:
  Rahab against Jericho   *Josh. 2:1–21*
  Absalom against David   *2 Sam. 15:1–14*
  Athaliah against Judah   *2 Kings 11*

Treasure (See also Riches)
- Figurative of:
  New life in Jesus Christ   *2 Cor. 4:6–7*
  Wisdom   *Prov. 2:4*
  Spiritual understanding   *Matt. 13:52; Col. 2:2–3*
  Tabernacle used for   *Num. 31:54; Josh. 6:19–24*
  Solomon's temple used for   *1 Kings 7:51*

Tree (See also Branch)
- Figurative of:
  Righteous   *Ps. 1:1–3*
  Works of righteous   *Prov. 11:30*
  Wisdom   *Prov. 3:18*
  Eternal life   *Gen. 3:22, 24; Rev. 22:14*

Trial (See also Adversity, Affliction, Discipline)
Test and prove faith   *Gen. 22:1–14*
Purify faith   *1 Pet. 1:6–9*
Suffered as Christian   *1 Pet. 4:12–16*
Develops perseverance   *James 1:3*
Sometimes severe   *2 Cor. 1:8–11*

Tribes of Israel
Named for 12 sons of Jacob   *Gen. 49*

Tribulation (See also Adversity, Suffering, Trouble)

In the world   *John 16:33; Acts 14:22*
To increase in the end times   *Matt. 24:21*
Results in patience   *Rom. 5:3*
Known by God   *Rev. 2:9*

Trinity (See also God, Holy Spirit, Jesus Christ)

Revealed at Jesus' baptism   *Matt. 3:16–17*
Jesus commanded to baptize in name of   *Matt. 28:19*
■ Same work attributed to three members of:
   Creation   *Gen. 1:1; Ps. 104:30; Col. 1:16*
   Salvation   *2 Thess. 2:13–14; Titus 3:4–6; 1 Pet. 1:2*

Troas

Where Paul had vision   *Acts 16:8–9*

Trouble (See also Adversity, Affliction, Temptation)

As test of faith   *James 1:2–3; 1 Pet. 1:7*
As judgment   *Ps. 107:17*
As sign of God's love   *Heb. 12:5–6*
God is faithful in   *Rom. 8:35–39*
God comforts those in   *Matt. 5:4*
Believers should be patient in   *1 Pet. 2:20*

Trumpet

■ Will be sounded at:
   Christ's coming   *Matt. 24:31; 1 Thess. 4:16*
   Judgment   *Rev. 8:2, 13*

Trust (See also Belief, Confidence, Faith)

With whole heart   *Prov. 3:5*
■ In the Lord:
   Forever   *Isa. 26:4*
   For peace   *Isa. 26:3*
   For safety   *Prov. 29:25*

In the Word of God   Ps. 119:42
Not in man   Ps. 118:89; Jer. 17:5
Not in wealth   Prov. 11:28; Luke 12:19–20

Truth (See also Honesty, Integrity, Truthfulness)
Attribute of God   Isa. 65:16
Spirit of   John 15:26
Christ is   John 14:6
Word of God is   John 17:17
Church is bulwark of   1 Tim. 3:15
Believing the   2 Thess. 2:12

Truthfulness (See also Deceit, Honesty, Truth)
In speech   Prov. 12:19
In witness   Prov. 14:25
Speaking to one another in   Zech. 8:16
Christ became a servant to show   Rom. 15:8

Tychicus
Companion of Paul   Acts 20:4; 2 Tim. 4:12; Titus 3:12
Commended   Eph. 6:21; Col. 4:7

Type (See also Symbol)
Adam   Rom. 5:14
Melchizedek   Heb. 7:1–17
Paschal Lamb   1 Cor. 5:7
Tabernacle   Heb. 8:5
Bride   Rev. 21:2, 9; 22:17

Tyranny (See also Government)
■ Judged by God:
Poor avenged   Isa. 1:23–25
Oppressor exiled   Hos. 5:10
God spoke against   Ezek. 45:9
God will abandon those guilty of   Mic. 3:1–4

Tyre
Its wealth and fall   Ezek. 26:7–28:19

U

Unbelief (See also Belief, Unbeliever)
In Word of God Ps. 106:24; John 5:38
In miracles Num. 14:11-12; John 12:37
A cry to overcome Mark 9:24
Judgment against 2 Thess. 2:12; Jude 5
Warning against John 3:36; Heb. 3:12

Unbeliever (See also Belief, Disciple, Heathen)
■ Paul speaks about:
  Lawsuits against 1 Cor. 6:6
  Reaction to speaking in tongues 1 Cor. 14:23
  Marriage to 2 Cor. 6:14
Mind and conscience are corrupt Titus 1:15
Is condemned John 3:18

Uncleanness (See also Cleanliness, Purity)
Ceremonial Lev. 13:3, 14, 25
Caused by touching Lev. 11:8; Acts 10:11-14
Comes from within Matt. 15:11, 18
Is sin Eph. 4:19

Understanding (See also Knowledge, Wisdom)
Man lacking Ps. 14:1-4; Rom. 3:11
Blessing of Prov. 3:13-15
Asking for Ps. 119:27
■ Given by God to:
  Bezalel Exod. 31:1-3
  Solomon 1 Kings 3:12

Unfaithfulness (See also Backsliding, Idolatry, Loyalty)
Judgment of Matt. 3:10; 21:43
Parables of Isa. 5:1-7; Mark 12:1-9
■ Examples of:
  By leaders Jer. 6:13-15

By Israel   *Hos. 4:1*

Unity (See also Communion of Saints, Fellowship)
- Of believers:
  In Christ   *John 15:4-7; 1 Cor. 3:23; Gal. 2:20*
  In Church   *Gal. 3:28*
  In mind and spirit   *1 Cor. 1:10; Phil. 1:27; 1 Pet. 3:8*
- Illustrated by:
  Body   *Rom. 12:4-5; 1 Cor. 10:17*
  Husband and wife   *Eph. 5:25-32*

Unpardonable Sin (See also Forgiveness)
Blasphemy against Holy Spirit   *Matt. 12:31-32; Mark 3:29*

Unselfishness (See also Humility, Love)
In living   *Matt. 16:24-25; 1 Cor. 10:24*
In true love   *1 Cor. 13:4-5*
- Examples of:
  Abraham   *Gen. 13:8-9*
  David   *1 Chron. 21:17*
  Paul   *1 Cor. 9:12-22; 10:33*
  Christ   *Mark 6:30-34; Rom. 15:1-3*

Ur
Land of Abraham's birth   *Gen. 11:28; 15:7*

Uriah
The Hittite, husband of Bathsheba   *2 Sam. 11:2-3*
Killed by David's order   *2 Sam. 11:14-17*

Uzziah
King of Judah   *2 Chron. 26:1-23*
Instructed by Zechariah   *2 Chron. 26:5*
Pride caused his downfall   *2 Chron. 26:16-21*

V

Vanity (See also Pride)
Thoughts are   *Rom. 1:21; Eph. 4:17–19*
Results from the fall   *Rom. 8:20*
Is the state of every man   *Ps. 62:9; 39:5–6*
Days of man are   *Job 7:16; Eccles. 1:2; 2:21*

Veil
- Of Tabernacle and Temple:
  To conceal Holy of Holies   *Exod. 40:3*
  Described   *Exod. 26:31–33*
  Torn at Christ's death   *Matt. 27:51*
- Figurative of:
  Spiritual blindness   *2 Cor. 3:14–16*
  The flesh of Christ   *Heb. 10:20*

Vengeance (See also Retaliation, Revenge)
Forbidden to man   *Matt. 5:38–39*
Belongs to God   *Deut. 32:35; Prov. 20:22*
On disobedient nations   *Mic. 5:15*

Victory (See also Battle, Joy, Overcoming)
God assured   *Deut. 20:4*
God gave to David   *2 Sam. 8:6; 1 Chron. 18:6*
Brought joy   *Ps. 20:5*
Belongs to the Lord   *Prov. 21:31*
Over death   *1 Cor. 15:54*
Through faith   *1 John 5:4*

V

Vine (See also Agriculture, Branch)
Fruitfulness of   *Joel 2:22*
Unfruitfulness of   *Jer. 8:13*
- Figurative of:
  Israel's unfaithfulness   *Ps. 80:8–19*
  Christ and believers   *John 15*
  Judgment   *Ezek. 15:6; Rev. 14:18–19*

Virgin (See also Celibacy, Chastity)

Remaining as a   1 Cor. 7:25-26
- Figurative of:
  Israel   Jer. 14:17
  Church   2 Cor. 11:2
  Believers   Matt. 25:1-9
- Birth:
  Prophesied   Isa. 7:14
  Fulfilled   Matt. 1:23, 25

Virtue (See also Character, Goodness, Righteousness)

Resulting from faith   2 Pet. 1:5
Christians possess   Rom. 15:14; Gal. 5:22

Vision (See also Dream, Eye, Revelation)

Of true prophets   Joel 2:28
Of false prophets   Jer. 14:14; 23:16
- Examples of:
  Jacob   Gen. 46:2
  Prophets   Isa. 6; Dan. 7
  The Apostle John   Rev. 1:9-20

Vocation (See also Calling, Career, Work)

Living worthy of   Eph. 4:1

Voice (See also Singing, Speech)

- Of God:
  Powerful   Job 40:9; Ps. 68:33
  Whisper   1 Kings 19:12
  From heaven   Matt. 3:17; 17:5; Acts 9:4-6

Vow (See also Oath, Promise)

- Made to God:
  Example of   Gen. 28:20
  Should be fulfilled   Num. 30:2; Deut. 23:21
To be taken with care   Prov. 20:25

W

Waiting (See also Impatience, Patience)
- Upon God:
  Encouraged   *Ps. 27:14*
  Blessing of   *Isa. 40:31*
For promise of God   *Acts 1:4*
For coming of Christ   *1 Cor. 1:7; 1 Thess. 1:10*
For fulfillment of God's words   *Hab. 2:3*
For guidance and teaching   *Ps. 25:5*

Walk (See also Conversation, Way)
With God   *Gen. 5:24· 6:9*
- Figurative:
  Before God   *Gen. 17:1; Ps. 116:9*
  In light   *1 John 1:7*
  In love   *Eph. 5:2*
  In the spirit   *Gal. 5:16*
  In new life   *Rom. 6:4*
  In truth   *2 John 4; 3 John 3*

Wall (See also Protection)
- Of Cities:
  Destruction caused grief   *Deut. 28:52; Neh. 1:3;
     1 Kings 20:30*
- Figurative of:
  Salvation   *Isa. 26:1; 60:18*
  Separation   *Eph. 2:13-14*
  Hypocrites   *Acts 23:3*

War (See also Armor, Army, Battle)
Originates in lust of men   *James 4:1-2*
Victory given by God   *Num. 21:3*
As a judgment of God   *2 Kings 15:37*
To cease   *Isa. 2:4*
Horrors of   *Ps. 79:1-4*
Figurative of Christian life   *2 Cor. 10:3; Eph. 6:12*

Washing (See also Bathing, Cleansing, Purification)
Ceremonial   *Exod. 29:4*
- Figurative of sins:
  By God   *Isa. 1:18; Eph. 5:26*
  Asking for   *Ps. 51:7*
  By blood of Christ   *1 John 1:7*
Of feet   *Luke 7:44; John 13:5*
Of hands   *Ps. 26:6; Matt. 27:24*

Watchfulness (See also Waiting)
Against sin   *Matt. 26:41*
For Second Coming   *Matt. 25:13; 1 Thess. 5:6; Rev. 16:15*
- Characterized by:
  Prayer   *Eph. 6:18*
  Steadfastness   *1 Cor. 16:13*

Water (See also Life, Purity, Thirst)
- Figurative:
  Of affliction   *Ps. 42:7; Isa. 30:20*
  Of life   *Rev. 7:17; John 4:10; 7:37–38*
  Of Holy Spirit   *John 7:38–39; Isa. 44:3*
Miracles involving   *Exod. 14:21; John 2:9*

Wave Offering (See also Offering)
Given to Priests   *Exod. 29:26–28; Lev. 7:31, 34*
To be eaten in a holy place   *Lev. 10:14*
- Offered for:
  Consecration of priests   *Lev. 8:29*
  Jealousy   *Num. 5:25*
  Leper's trespass   *Lev. 14:1, 12*

Way (See also Road, Walk)
- Figurative of:
  Christ   *John 14:6; Heb. 10:20*
  The wicked   *Ps. 35:6; Prov. 4:19; 15:9*
To life   *Isa. 26:7; Matt. 7:14*

That is perfect   *Ps. 18:30; Dan. 4:37*
Above man's   *Isa. 55:9; Rom. 11:33*
Guidance for   *Prov. 3:6; Isa. 42:16*
Descriptive of early Christians   *Acts 19:19*

Weakness (See also Strength)
■ Of Men:
  Caused by sin   *Josh. 7:12; Mark 9:18*
  Cared for by God   *Ps. 116:6*
  Leads to dependency on God   *2 Cor. 3:5*
  Christ sympathetic with   *Heb. 4:15*
Of God stronger than men   *1 Cor. 1:25*

Wealth (See Money, Riches)

Weapon (See also Armor, Battle)
Wisdom better than   *Eccles. 9:18*
Shall be destroyed   *Ezek. 39:9–10*
■ Figurative of:
  Nations   *Jer. 51:20*
  Righteousness   *2 Cor. 6:7*
  Divine power   *2 Cor. 10:4*
  God's wrath   *Isa. 13:5; Jer. 50:25*

Weeping (See also Grief, Sorrow, Tear)
In grief   *Gen. 21:16; 1 Sam. 1:6–8; Acts 20:37*
Caused by sin   *Deut. 1:45; Jer. 3:21*
In hell   *Matt. 8:12; 24:51*
Leads to joy   *Ps. 30:5; Luke 6:21*
At tomb of Christ   *John 20:15*

Weights and Measures
Fairness in   *Lev. 19:35, 36; Prov. 11:1*

Welfare (See also Charity, Poor People, Society)
■ Of God's people:
  God delights in   *Ps. 35:27*
  Jeremiah accused of not caring for   *Jer. 38:4*

Abundant in following wisdom   *Prov. 3:1-2*
God's concern for the poor and oppressed   *Prov.
14:31; Isa. 58:6-11*

Wheat (See also Agriculture)
In offerings   *Num. 18:12; 1 Chron. 21:23*
Parable of   *Matt. 13:25; Luke 16:7*

Wheel
Used to thresh grain   *Isa. 28:27*
Of potter   *Jer. 18:3*
Symbolic   *Ezek. 1:15-21; 3:13; 10:9-19; 11:22*
Figurative of life ending   *Eccles. 12:6*

White (See also Color)
■ Descriptive of:
  Clothing   *Matt. 17:2; Rev. 3:5; 4:4*
  Angels   *Matt. 28:3; Acts 1:10*
  Harvest   *John 4:35*
■ Symbolic of:
  Cleansing from sin   *Isa. 1:18; Dan. 12:10*
  Purity   *Rev. 2:17; 6:2*

Wickedness (See also Abomination, Evil, Sin)
Suppresses truth   *Rom. 1:18*
Detested   *Prov. 8:7*
Brings wrath of God   *Gen. 6:5-7; Isa. 9:18-19*
Becomes object of reproach   *Ezek. 16:56-58*

Widow (See also Orphan)
Allowed to glean fields   *Deut. 24:19; Ruth 2:2*
Oppression of forbidden   *Exod. 22:22; Zech. 7:10*
May remarry   *1 Cor. 7:39; 1 Tim. 5:11-15*
Levitical laws concerning   *Deut. 24:19; Ruth 3:10-13*
■ Provision for:
  By God   *Deut. 10:18; Prov. 15:25*
  By church   *Acts 6:1-3; 1 Tim. 5:9*
  By relatives   *1 Tim. 5:16*

Wife (See also Husband, Marriage)
Becomes one with husband   *Gen. 2:24; Matt. 19:5-6*
Blessing from God   *Prov. 12:4; 18:22*
Duties of   *Prov. 31:27; Titus 2:4-5*
■ Should:
  Be modest   *1 Tim. 2:9*
  Do good   *1 Tim. 2:10; 5:10*
  Have a quiet spirit   *1 Pet. 3:4-5*

Wilderness
Place of testing   *Mark 1:12; Heb. 3:8*
Place of refuge   *1 Sam. 26:3; Luke 4:42; Rev. 12:6*
Voice in   *Isa. 40:3; Matt. 3:3*
Made fruitful   *Isa. 41:18*

Will, Last Testament
Of Abraham   *Gen. 25:5-6*
Of Jacob   *Gen. 48:3-49:28*
Of David   *1 Kings 2:1-9*
Not to be annulled   *Gal. 3:15*
Enforced after death   *Heb. 9:16-17*

Will of God (See also Guidance, Predestination)
Christ's resignation to   *Matt. 26:39; John 6:38-39*
Asking for   *Matt. 6:10*
Directing early missions   *Acts 18:21; Rom. 15:30-32*
That Christians abstain from immorality   *1 Thess. 4:3*

Will of Man (See also Self-will)
Free to choose good or evil   *Josh. 24:15; Deut. 30:19*
In bondage to sin   *Prov. 5:22; Rom. 6:16*
Set free by Christ   *2 Tim. 2:26*
To be inclined towards God   *Deut. 5:29; Isa. 1:19*

Wind (See also Spirit, Holy Spirit)
Providential   *Gen. 8:1*
Of pestilence   *Jer. 4:11*

■ Miracles with:
Bringing locusts   *Exod. 10:13, 19*
Calmed by Christ   *Matt. 8:26-27; 14:32*
■ Figurative of:
Life of men   *Job 7:7*
Work of Spirit   *Ezek. 37:9; John 3:8;*
False doctrine   *James 1:6*

Wine (See also Drinking, Drunkenness, Vine)
For enjoyment   *Ps. 104:15*
Water turned into   *John 2:9*
■ In excess:
Forbidden   *Eph. 5:18*
Leads to sorrow   *Prov. 23:29-30*
■ Symbolic of:
Blood of Christ   *Matt. 26:27-29*
Judgment of God   *Ps. 60:3; Jer. 13:12-14*

Wisdom (See also Knowledge, Learning, Philosophy)
Christ as believers'   *1 Cor. 1:30; Col. 2:3*
Value of   *Job 28:12-28; Prov. 8:11; Eccles. 7:19*
Given by God   *Eccles. 2:26; James 1:5*
Prayers for   *2 Chron. 1:10; Ps. 90:12; Eph. 1:17*
Characteristic of Christ   *Matt. 13:54; Luke 2:40*
Personified   *Prov. 8:1*

Witchcraft (See also Astrology, Magic, Occult)
A sin   *Lev. 19:31; 20:6; Gal. 5:20*
Practitioners to be destroyed   *Exod. 22:18; Mic. 5:12*
Is vain   *Isa. 8:19; 19:3-4*
■ Examples of:
Witch of Endor   *1 Sam. 28:7*
Jezebel   *2 Kings 9:22*

Witness (See also Apostle, Evangelism, Witnessing)
Christian to be a   *Acts 1:8*

- Of Holy Spirit:
  To Christ   *John 15:26; Acts 5:32; 1 John 5:8*
  Given to believers   *Acts 15:8; Rom. 8:16;*
      1 John 3:24
Two required   *Num. 35:30; Matt. 18:16*
Corrupted by money   *Matt. 28:11-15; Acts 36:11-14*

Witnessing (See also Evangelism, Witness)
Paul before King Agrippa   *Acts 26:22*
As a Christian   *1 Pet. 3:15*
- Examples of:
  Andrew   *John 1:40-42*
  Woman at the well   *John 4:28-30*
  John the Baptist   *John 3:27, 31-36*

Woman (See also Man, Wives, Motherhood)
Creation of   *Gen. 1:27; 2:21-23*
Devout   *1 Sam. 1:15; Luke 1:25; Rom. 16:1*
Believers, heirs with Christ   *Gal. 3:26-29*

Word of God (See also Scripture)
Given by inspiration   *1 Cor. 2:12; 2 Tim. 3:16;*
    2 Pet. 1:21
Testifies to Jesus Christ   *John 5:39; 20:30; Heb. 1:1*
Faithful and true   *Rev. 22:6*
Eternal   *Mark 13:31*
To hear and understand   *Matt. 13:23*
Obeying it brings blessing   *Luke 11:28*
- Compared to:
  A sword   *Eph. 6:17; Heb. 4:12*
  Seed   *Luke 8:11*

Work (See also Business, Career, Vocation)
- Physical:
  Forbidden on Sabbath   *Exod. 23:12; Deut. 5:12-13*
  Be diligent in   *Eccles. 9:10; Col. 3:23; 1 Thess. 4:11*
- Religious:
  Illustrated by parables   *Matt. 21:28; 25:21*

Of the Lord   *1 Cor. 15:58*
Of salvation   *Eph. 2:8-10; Phil. 2:12-13*
With God's help   *Rom. 8:26; 1 Cor. 3:6-9;
    2 Cor. 6:1*

Works (See also Faith)

■ Good:
Not for salvation   *Matt. 7:22; Rom. 3:20; Eph. 2:8-9*
Encouraged in Christians   *Matt. 5:16; Titus 2:7;
    1 Pet. 2:12*
Belief in Christ   *John 6:28-29*
■ Of God:
Are good   *Gen. 1:10, 18, 21*
Unsearchable and great   *Ps. 40:5; 92:4; 136:4*
Of evil   *John 7:7; James 3:14-16; Jude 14-16*
Judging of   *Ps. 62:12; Matt. 16:27; 2 Cor. 5:10*

World (See also Creation, Earth)

Creation of   *Gen. 1:1; Job 26:7; Heb. 11:3*
End of   *Isa. 34:4; 2 Pet. 3:10-11; Rev. 21:1*
Will pass   *Ps. 102:25-26; 1 Cor. 7:31; 2 Cor. 4:18*
As God's footstool   *Isa. 66:1; Matt. 5:35; Acts 7:49*
System, separation from commanded   *Rom. 12:2;
    Eph. 5:11; 1 John 2:15*

Worldliness (See also Bad Company, Sin, World)

Imitation of the godless   *1 Sam. 8:19-20; Eph. 2:2*
Warnings against   *Matt. 12:26; Col. 3:2; Titus 2:12*
■ Effects of:
Unbelief   *Matt. 13:22; Col. 2:8; 2 Tim. 4:10*
Delusion   *Matt. 24:38-39*
Unprofitable   *Eccles. 2:11; Matt. 6:19; Luke 9:25*

Worry (See also Anxiety, Care, Stress)

Lack of trust in God   *Matt. 6:31-32, 34*
Chokes spiritual life   *Matt. 13:22*
Forbidden   *Matt. 6:25; Luke 21:34; Phil. 4:6*
Cast upon Christ   *1 Pet. 5:7*

Worship (See also Praise, Prayer, Thanksgiving)

Of God, commanded   *Exod. 20:3; Deut. 5:7;*
    Matt. 4:10
Of Christ   *John 9:38; Heb. 1:6; Rev. 5:8–9*
Attitude in   *Lev. 10:3; Ps. 5:7; John 4:24*
Universal   *Ps. 22:27; Rom. 14:11; Phil. 2:9–10*
Places of   *Jer. 26:2; Acts 1:13–14; Col. 4:15*

Wrath (See also Anger, Punishment)

■ Of God:
  Against the disobedient   *Rom. 1:18; 2:8; Eph. 5:6*
  Against unbelief   *John 3:36*
Of man, forbidden   *Ps. 37:8; Eph. 4:26; James 1:19*
Cup of   *Jer. 25:15; Rev. 14:10*

Writing (See also Scribe)

On stone   *Deut. 27:3; Josh. 8:32*
■ On paper:
  The Law   *Deut. 31:9*
  Documents   *1 Sam. 10:25; 1 Chron. 9:1*
On the heart   *Prov. 3:3; 7:3; Jer. 31:33; Heb. 8:10*

X, Y, Z

Xerxes (See Ahasuerus)

Years (See also Day, Season)
Sabbatical   *Exod. 23:11; Lev. 25:4*
Jubilee   *Lev. 25:10, 28; 27:17; Num. 36:4; Ezek. 46:17*
■ One thousand:
  Satan bound   *Rev. 20:2-4, 7*
  As a day to God   *Ps. 90:4; 2 Pet. 3:8*

Yoke (See also Bondage, Discipline, Punishment)
■ Figurative of:
  Oppression of kings   *1 Kings 12:4-14*
  Oppression of nations   *Jer. 28:1-14*
  Sin   *Lam. 1:14*
Of Christ   *Matt. 11:29-30*

Youth (See also Adolescence, Children, Old Age)
Not to be despised   *2 Tim. 4:12*
Remember God in   *Eccles. 12:1*
■ Examples of calling in:
  David   *1 Sam. 17:33*
  Jeremiah   *Jer. 1:4-8*
  Samuel   *1 Sam. 3:10-4:1*
Sins of   *Ps. 25:7; Jer. 32:30*

Zaccheus
Wanted to see Jesus   *Luke 19:2*

Zachariah, Zechariah
King of Israel   *2 Kings 14:29*
Prophet   *Zech. 1:1*

Zacharias
Father of John the Baptist   *Luke 1:6*
Struck dumb by angel for doubting   *Luke 1:18, 22*

Zadok
Priest who anointed Solomon   1 Kings 1:39

Zeal
Of God   2 Kings 19:31; Isa. 26:11; 37:32
■ Religious:
  Encouraged   1 Thess. 2:11–12
  For Law   Acts 21:20
Misguided   Rom. 10:2
■ Exemplified by:
  Moses   Exod. 2:12, 11:8; 32:19–20
  Jesus   John 2:17; Acts 10:38
  Paul   Acts 32:3

Zebulun
Coming of Messiah there prophesied and fulfilled
    Isa. 9:1, 6–7; Matt. 4:13

Zedekiah (Mattaniah)
King of Judah   2 Kings 24:17; 25:1–7

Zephaniah
Prophesied during reign of Josiah   Zeph. 1:1

Zerubbabel
Prince of Judah   Ezra 2:2

Zion (See also Jerusalem, Kingdom)
Fortress captured by David   2 Sam. 5:6–9
Dwelling place of God   Isa. 8:18
■ Figurative of:
  Israel as God's people   2 Kings 19:21
  Kingdom of God   Ps. 125:1
  City of God   Heb. 12:22
  Heaven   Rev. 14:1

X
Y
Z

Other Pocketpac Books

PERSONAL PROMISE POCKETBOOK. Discover how God's promises and purposes correspond to many of your needs. The Four-Step system will help you claim and retain these verses.

STUDENT PROMISE POCKETBOOK. A topical arrangement of verses to meet the specific needs of students and young adults.

PROMISES FOR THE GOLDEN YEARS. Special verses to fit the unique circumstances of older people. In large print!

PROMISES & PRAYERS FOR HEALING: Hope for the Future. Provides encouragement and hope for hurting people who desire God's healing touch.

More Books for Christian Living

CLOSER THAN A BROTHER. David Winter's reinterpretation of Brother Lawrence's *Practicing the Presence of God*.

GROWING IN HIS IMAGE by Bernard Bangley. Modern paraphrase of *The Imitation of Christ* by Thomas à Kempis.

THE HIDDEN BATTLE: Strategies for Spiritual Victory by David Watson. Gives Christians reinforcement for their battle with the world, the flesh, and the devil.

HOW TO LISTEN WHEN GOD SPEAKS by Chuck and Winnie Christensen. Practical helps for those who want to spend time with God and his Word each day.

Order from your favorite bookstore or write:
Harold Shaw Publishers, Box 567, Wheaton, Ill. 60189